MAKING SENSE OF LEADERSHIP

Exploring the five key roles used by effective leaders

Esther Cameron & Mike Green

**KOGAN
PAGE**

London and Philadelphia

Publisher's note

Every possible effort has been made to ensure that the information contained in this book is accurate at the time of going to press, and the publishers and authors cannot accept responsibility for any errors or omissions, however caused. No responsibility for loss or damage occasioned to any person acting, or refraining from action, as a result of the material in this publication can be accepted by the editor, the publisher or any of the authors.

First published in Great Britain and the United States in 2008 by Kogan Page Limited

120 Pentonville Road
London N1 9JN
United Kingdom
www.koganpage.com

525 South 4th Street, #241
Philadelphia PA 19147
USA

© Esther Cameron and Mike Green, 2008

ISBN 978 0 7494 5039 7

British Library Cataloguing-in-Publication Data

A CIP record for this book is available from the British Library.

Library of Congress Cataloging-in-Publication Data

Cameron, Esther.
    Making sense of leadership : exploring the five key roles used by effective leaders / Esther Cameron and Mike Green.
        p. cm.
    Includes bibliographical references and index.
    ISBN 978–0–7494–5039–7
    1. Leadership.   I. Green, Mike, 1959– II. Title
    HD57.7C3537 2008
    658.4'092--dc22
                                        2008017600

Typeset by Saxon Graphics Ltd, Derby
Printed and bound in India by Replika Press Pvt Ltd

Contents

MAKING

9. The Thoughtful Architect 84

The Thoughtful Architect role in a nutshell 85; All about the Thoughtful Architect role 86; The heart and soul of the Thoughtful Architect 86; The Thoughtful Architect's inner experience 87; The Thoughtful Architect's outer presentation 88; Organizational aspects of Thoughtful Architects 89; Examples of Thoughtful Architects 90

PART 3 THE RESEARCH 95

10. What roles do effective leaders use? 97

Objectives of the research 97; Research group 97; Roles used by effective leaders 98; Are the roles independent of each other? 100; What type of leader are you? 103; Which of the five roles do you find hardest to adopt? 104; Which of the five roles is most attractive as a role model? 106; Which of the roles would you least like to be led by? 108; Which are the most and least prevalent styles in your organization? 109; Conclusions 110

11. Which roles are needed when? 112

Restructuring 114; Crisis 115; Technology-led change 116; Process re-engineering 117; Merger, acquisition or takeover 118; Working with partners and stakeholders 119; Improving supply chain management 120; Growing a new enterprise 120; Unhappy workforce 121; New product or service to be designed and launched 122; New legislation, tighter compliance and critical project – well-defined change 122; Complex whole-organization change, cultural change and working towards a five-year strategy – long-range complex change 123; Well-defined change versus long-range complex change 124

Acknowledgements

This book is a heartfelt attempt to encourage people who want to become better leaders to play a bit more. Experimentation and spontaneity are becoming harder and harder to find in this fast, busy and highly target-oriented world. As we grow more sophisticated in our approaches to leadership, and consequently more pre-programmed in our methods, so the opportunity to break out of set ways of doing things becomes more necessary, but somehow more difficult to do. Our experience is that learning sessions which involve playing with different options through exaggeration, improvisation and even deliberate mistake-making are much more productive than traditional round the table discussion. When it comes to developing true leadership skills, analysis and logic just don't hit the spot. There is nothing like a live experiment to bring out the best in people.

The ideas in this book may appear simple and obvious, but they took a great deal of talking and trying out before they became crystallized in this form. Many people were involved along the way.

We want to first thank all those wonderful people who filled in questionnaires. Thanks also to the colleagues and clients who listened to our enthusiastic ramblings, tried out our strange leadership exercises, allowed us to observe and document their leadership styles and who read and commented on our disconnected pieces of writing. Thanks to all of you for your generous donations of time and energy.

Louise Overy's exacting editing of the text was absolutely fundamental to this book being in the shape it's in. She made some great creative suggestions and asked piercing questions about the point of it all, as well as picking through the minutiae of our less than competent use of English. Thanks also go to Hugh Swan, who created an online version of our questionnaire in an incredibly short timescale and to Jeff Piggott whose elegantly drawn figures grace these pages.

Thanks very much also to Ron Wiener, our guide to the world of sociodrama, for introducing us to the possibility that learning a new role could be spontaneous and fun. Have a look at his courses at www.mpv-sam.com if you want to be similarly inspired.

Huge thanks must also go to Mary Hughes from Public Services Management Wales for letting us loose on the public sector managers of Wales to try out our ideas and to get a lovely chunk of research data. Thanks also to the other excellent people in our network of leaders who were kind enough to fill in various fumbling versions of questionnaires prior to the final version.

Several people have been significant playful spirits and inspirational presences along the way. Susan Weil, Professor Emeritus at UWE, first introduced us to the world of live systemic exploration, and the use of sociodramatic approaches. Barry Oshry's use of drama-based methods to understand and explore issues of power and hierarchy has been highly influential too, as has Nick Mayhew's pioneering use of dramatic provocations to prick the consciences of business people interested in sustainable development.

A personal note from Esther: Thanks to Duncan for offering both calm support and an incredible willingness to step seamlessly into the homemaker role while I fiddled about in my office, allegedly thinking. Thank you also to my children Ailsa and Ewan, for reminding me in the nicest possible way that I'm human and fallible, for being great role models for spontaneity and creativity and, best of all, for helping me to laugh out loud almost every day.

And from Mike: Thanks to family and friends and work colleagues and of course, Esther, all of whom have been incredibly supportive during the writing of the book, before and after. Time spent researching and writing inevitably means sacrificing and losing other things. Hopefully any loss will be made good over time.

Now it's your journey. Enjoy it.

Esther Cameron	Mike Green
www.cameronchange.co.uk	www.transitionalspace.co.uk
esther@cameronchange.co.uk	mike@transitionalspace.co.uk

Please keep a look out on both our websites for slide packs, trainer guides and workshop paraphernalia, which are all currently under development.

Part 1

Introduction

Leading from the inside out

When you step into a leadership position, the world changes and things are never quite the same again. People begin to have great expectations of you, and you begin to take on a strange and wonderful new role in relation to others. Sometimes this happens from the inside out; a new role appears at your fingertips as if by magic. Perhaps a parent, or a previous boss, or a teacher has subtly invaded your psyche as a role model and you begin to take on their mantle. But maybe you lack the right role models, and you have to work at things a bit harder. You try to develop your leadership approach from the outside in. You read about how to lead, and you acquire leadership skills on a training course. You might even study the ideas behind leadership by taking an MBA and you find out about what great leaders do. But somehow this is never quite as powerful as learning from a role model. It's a lot harder, and can feel a bit fragmented; therefore it may come across as unconvincing or manufactured.

What we have tried to do in this book is to help you in this process of becoming a successful leader, by enabling you to identify the key roles that leaders take, and therefore to begin to lead from the inside out. So rather than list all the things that good leaders do, or examine impressive case studies of well-known leaders, we identify the natural clusters of behaviour that form patterned leadership roles. We have posed the question 'If successful organizational leaders were actors in a play, what roles would they typically take?' In short, we are putting today's organizational leadership archetypes under the spotlight. We have explored the core roles that successful leaders typically step into in order to lead well and make things happen, such as significant innovations and changes in direction that would not otherwise have happened. We believe that discovering these roles offers an important guide to the new leader, who is then more able to shape his or her own leadership approach according to situation and personality. It can also provide interesting challenges to the existing leader who wants to refresh his or her stance in order to tackle a new situation.

The approach that professional actors take to role development has influenced our thinking about the best way to learn a new leadership role. Uta Hagen, the great Broadway actress, made an important distinction between Representational acting and Presentational acting which we see as very relevant. She said that Representational actors seek to imitate a character's behaviours, and aim to reproduce an objective result. There is a slightly clinical air to this approach which can alienate the audience in subtle ways. Presentational actors, however, are different. These actors instead attempt to shed some light on human behaviour by understanding themselves and identifying with the character. Presentational actors trust that knowing the character well and understanding the motivations and situation of that character will help them to discover the role moment by moment on stage, in a subjective way. Hagen also remarks that Representational acting may be impressive and draw a large round of applause, but Presentational acting offers more empathy with human behaviour and engages the audience in a more authentic, emotional way.

> The Presentational actor... is different. This actor instead attempts to shed some light on human behaviour by understanding him/herself and identifying with the character. A Presentational actor trusts that knowing the character well and understanding the motivations and situation of that character will help him or her to discover the role moment by moment on stage, in a subjective way. (Uta Hagen, Broadway actress)

The disciplines and ideas behind sociodrama have influenced our thinking too, especially the notion that creativity and spontaneity are absolutely vital to our ability to adapt and learn, and to lead rich and joyful lives. Sociodrama is a spontaneous and unscripted group activity which allows people to explore the problems and issues of human relations that are relevant to them. Through the practice of sociodrama, people are offered the opportunity to experiment and play with roles that are completely outside their experience, or to play their current roles in very different ways; spontaneity and creativity are the cornerstones of sociodrama.

Jacob L Moreno, the founding father of sociodrama, was very interested in the way we are able to expand our ability to step into different roles ('role repertoire') and take on new ways of doing things. He noticed that when we take on a new role in life, we begin with a fairly rigid version of the role, and as we relax into the role we become more creative and spontaneous. He also remarked that one of the greatest dangers facing modern humanity is our habit of approaching tasks and interactions, especially in business, in a robotized and routine way, extinguishing all opportunities for spontaneity. He saw this as a threat to our collective state of mind, eventually leading to a joyless and unsatisfying existence as our ability to be experimental and risk-taking in the moment diminishes.

> Sociodrama is a spontaneous and unscripted group activity which allows people to explore the problems and issues of human relations that are relevant to them. Through the practice of sociodrama, people are offered the opportunity to experiment and play with roles that are completely outside their experience…

We are also interested in helping leaders to decide what role is best to take. How is it possible for them to find out what the organization needs from them in terms of leadership? Bookshops are full of texts on how to be a great leader, and most managers are full of advice for their staff about what type of leader they need to be, but we wondered whether there was some science to this. Do different situations require very different leadership approaches? This is intuitively the case, but we believe this has only really been explored in a one-to-one setting, rather than investigating the match between situation and successful leadership approach.

We believe leaders need to develop their capacity to tune into an organizational system and get a good sense of what the organization needs in terms of leadership, rather than do what they did last time, or do what the boss is telling them to do. By having a better sense of the approaches open to them, and the effects of these approaches, leaders have more real choice available when it comes to the crunch moments. And the crunch moments come more often than many leaders imagine.

We have therefore come up with five valuable leadership roles that leaders can experiment with as if they were making a recipe: a little bit of this and a little bit of that plus a huge dollop of this, according to who you're cooking for, your personal preference, the available ingredients and what sort of day and season of the year it is. We have introduced these roles to hundreds of managers in the UK and have discovered that people who are involved in managing or leading every day appear to 'get' the five roles very quickly. Our US colleagues have reported the same experience. They recognize these types and can place themselves and others very easily. Some people prefer to use just one of the roles. Many people use a mixture of different roles. Many people can identify at least one role that seems difficult for them to access.

We have found that leaders enjoy playing around with the five roles, either in conversation or in action, which we have encouraged them to do in our more experimental workshops. They then discover together with others which roles they typically take and with what frequency. They can experiment with the mix, try out different roles, or subtly change the way they typically respond. They can exaggerate particular roles, or parody them, and they can say the things they would never say and try things out in different situations. This type of live experimentation with the five roles is much more akin to the way people really learn than the cognitive methods used by traditional training courses. It's also more fun!

Leadership is about stepping forward and doing something that otherwise wouldn't be done. It's about putting your head above the parapet, or making your unique mark on a blank sheet of paper. Leadership is not a skill that can be acquired in a purely behavioural way by segmenting out coaching or presenting or influencing and then focusing on that in a purely cognitive sense. It's much deeper and broader than that. By experimenting in this way, leaders can start to widen their sense of what roles they can master, and therefore what they can achieve. The more we can allow individuals to recognize that leading is far more than applying a set of skills in a mechanistic manner the better and more successful organizations will be!

We intend, through this book, to debunk some of the myths that have built up about what makes a successful leader, which will in turn allow leaders to be more adventurous in their role-taking and encourage organizations to be more creative and broad-minded when appointing people into leadership roles. Leaders don't all have to be highly dominant people; they don't all have to be interpersonal wizards. It's not essential for all leaders to be electrifying speakers and leading-edge thinkers. Neither is it essential for every single leader to be superbly organized… but it does help to be at least some of these things. And leaders have to learn to develop the right mix of role to match their personality, the organizational situation and the people around them.

How to use this book

This book is divided into five parts, described below. The best way to approach this book is to read it in the order presented. However, if you are impatient to get started, you could go straight to the self-assessment chapter in Part 4 to find out which roles you use most frequently. Then you could return to Part 2 to read about the different roles. Then finally Part 4's chapter on stepping into a new role will help you to develop some radically new leadership approaches. This means skipping over the research and the theory, which we recommend you return to when you are less hurried.

PART 1: INTRODUCTION

Part 1 begins with the Introduction which explains what the book is about, what it is trying to achieve and why we thought it was an important book to write. Chapter 2 is entitled 'How to use this book', which is where you are right now. Chapter 3, 'The five roles – an overview' follows. This gives a first-level introduction to the roles that form the core of this book. Finally Chapter 4, 'Arriving at the five roles', will tell you all about where we started with our quest to find these roles and what sources we used to identify the five clusters of behaviours.

PART 2: UNDERSTANDING THE FIVE ROLES

Part 2 contains five chapters, each describing one of the five roles; Chapter 5 covers the Edgy Catalyser, Chapter 6 the Visionary Motivator, Chapter 7 the Measured Connector, Chapter 8 the Tenacious Implementer and Chapter 9 the Thoughtful Architect. For each role we first describe the heart of the role, which gives you a sense of the core values underpinning principles of the role. We then identify the inner experience and the outer presentation of each role, which will give you an idea about what you see from the outside as well as what is going on inside the individual who is taking this role. We go on to describe the organizational aspects of each role, identifying in which situations the role is most useful, and how this role might need to be adapted to particular organizational cultures. We also give real-life examples of each of the roles in action.

PART 3: THE RESEARCH

Part 3 is divided into two chapters, both based on data from our recent questionnaire completed by 83 experienced managers. Chapter 10, 'What roles do successful leaders use?', investigates how much the five leadership roles are being used by effective organizational leaders. It also investigates how distinctly different the fives roles are from each other, how people view these roles in terms of their effectiveness and attractiveness as a role model, and how difficult they find the roles to master. Chapter 11 is called 'What roles are needed when?' In this chapter we explore what combination of the five roles works best for a number of specific leadership challenges.

PART 4: EXPANDING YOUR ROLE REPERTOIRE

Part 4 provides leaders with a wide selection of tools and experiments that will help them to feel confident, creative and spontaneous in a range of leadership roles. Chapter 12 contains the self-assessment process which you can fill in to discover how often you tend to use each role. Next comes Chapter 13, entitled 'How to step into a new role', which explains some of the principles of how to expand your role repertoire and offers a checklist for each role. It also offers a wide range of exercises and quick tips for carrying out each role. In Chapter 14, 'The shadow side', there is an interesting exploration into the murky depths of leadership. Here we surface the more dysfunctional and extreme end of leadership behaviour and explain what precautions can be taken to mitigate against the dangerous effects of taking these leadership roles to extremes.

PART 5: RESOURCES FOR DEVELOPING OTHERS

Chapter 15 offers some ideas for facilitators and trainers who are running workshops or training courses and wish to experiment with some of the ideas in this book. Chapter 16 presents a brief analysis of each of the five leadership roles as they might be played out by people working in different types of job.

The five roles – an overview

Here's a brief overview of the five roles for those who want to get started quickly. For an in-depth description of each role, go to Part 2.

EDGY CATALYSER

The phrase which summarizes the stance of the Edgy Catalyser is: 'This is a serious problem. Can't you get some traction on this?' The key descriptors for the Edgy Catalyser are:

- asks the difficult, penetrating questions;
- spots dysfunction and resistance;
- creates discomfort and unease when things aren't improving.

How the Edgy Catalyser spends his or her time:

- going to see people;
- talking to people on the phone;

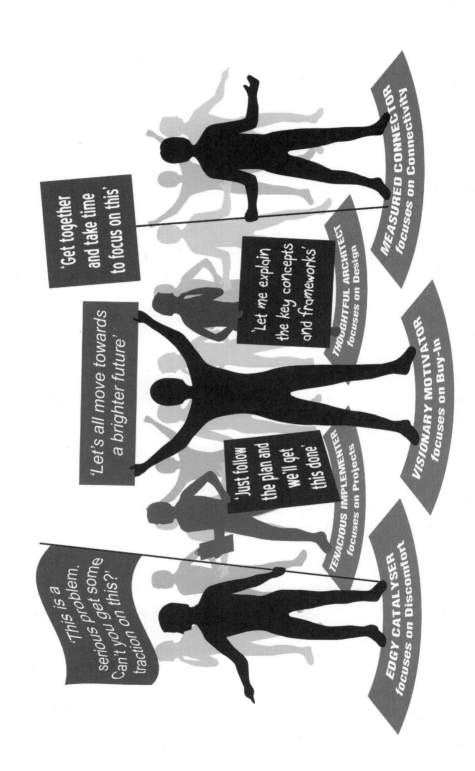

- analysing the facts;
- walking about, somewhere near the front line;
- having fierce conversations;
- being frank.

Best applications for the Edgy Catalyser:

- when something difficult needs to be faced;
- when there is a lot of pressure to change quickly;
- when traditions are getting in the way;
- when there is a crisis.

Well-known Edgy Catalysers:

- Hilary Clinton
- Alex Ferguson
- Sir Alan Sugar.

VISIONARY MOTIVATOR

The phrase which summarizes the stance of the Visionary Motivator is: 'Let's all move towards a brighter future.'
  The key descriptors for the Visionary Motivator are:

- articulates a compelling picture of the future;
- energizes groups of people and engages them;
- holds the vision long enough and strong enough for others to step into.

How the Visionary Motivator spends his or her time:

- in groups;
- talking energetically;
- with friends and colleagues;
- having dinner with people.

Best applications for the Visionary Motivator:

- when there is a big transition to make: cultural and strategic;
- when growth and risk-taking are needed;
- when morale is low.

Well-known Visionary Motivators:

- Tony Blair
- Howard Schultz
- Anita Roddick.

MEASURED CONNECTOR

The phrase which summarizes the stance of the Measured Connector is: 'Get together and take time to focus on this.'
   The key descriptors for the Measured Connector are:

- reinforces what's important and establishes a few simple rules;
- calmly influences complex change activity through focused reassurance;
- connects people and agendas.

How the Measured Connector spends his or her time:

- introducing people;
- reflecting either alone, or in small groups;
- talking about purpose;
- letting people know what the boundaries are;
- reaching out to stakeholders.

Best applications for the Measured Connector:

- to bring stakeholders and partners together;
- when morale is low;
- when cultural change is required;
- when the change is complex.

Well-known Measured Connectors:

- Sir Richard Branson
- Tim Smit
- Sven-Goran Eriksson.

TENACIOUS IMPLEMENTER

The phrase which summarizes the stance of the Tenacious Implementer is: 'Just follow the plan and we'll get this done.'
   The key descriptors for the Tenacious Implementer are:

- doggedly pursues the plan;
- holds people to account;
- leads by driving a project through to completion.

How the Tenacious Implementer spends his or her time:

- studying the plan;
- asking people where they are on the plan;
- coaching people (fairly forcibly);
- re-planning (reluctantly);
- calling teams together to discuss progress;
- influencing the key customer.

Best applications for Tenacious Implementer:

- critical projects;
- legislation and compliance challenges;
- technology-led change.

Well-known Tenacious Implementers:

- Vladimir Putin
- Michael Dell
- Gordon Brown.

THOUGHTFUL ARCHITECT

The phrase which summarizes the stance of the Thoughtful Architect is: 'Let me explain the key concepts and frameworks.'
   The key descriptors for the Thoughtful Architect are:

- is principal architect and designer of the strategies;
- crafts seemingly disparate ideas into a way forward;
- scans the environment, sees what's happening in the environment and creates an organizing framework.

How the Thoughtful Architect spends his or her time:

- thinking;
- reading;
- talking one to one with trusted confidants;
- sketching out designs;
- musing over options;
- occasionally presenting a grand plan (carefully prepared).

Best applications for the Thoughtful Architect:

- complex organizational change;
- long-range strategic change;
- difficult process change.

Well-known Thoughtful Architects:

- George Soros
- Bill Gates
- Albert Einstein.

4

Arriving at the five roles

INTRODUCTION

When we started to dig deep into what we really thought leadership was all about, specifically to write what we hoped would be a definitive book on the subject, we went back to basics. We gathered up all the models and ideas on leadership that we had been influenced by, impressed by, and even irritated by, and mapped them out on flipcharts all around our office. We then asked ourselves two questions. The first was 'What do successful leaders pay attention to?', and the second was 'What do successful leaders do?'

To answer these questions, we looked at leadership traits which formed the cradle of leadership ideas in the UK and the United States, then we gathered up all the materials we could get our hands on regarding leadership attitudes and styles as they were explored by the management researchers of the 1970s, such as Blake and Mouton. We also included the well-used situational leadership model and the work of Meredith Belbin on team roles. John Adair's team–task–individual model was there too (2004). We mapped out Goleman's six leadership styles with the supporting emotional intelligence competences, and included the works of Bennis and Kotter which usefully distinguish management from leadership. Stephen Covey was also present on our flipcharts. Some of the ideas of authentic leadership were there too, together with Margaret Wheatley's contributions on the importance of self-organization in healthy sustainable organizations.

We also added some 'real-world' examples into the pot, taking six sets of leadership competences gleaned from client organizations, many of which had been home grown, and some of which had been derived from existing academic materials.

Our aim was to cluster and group these ideas on leadership into four or five key leadership roles for 21st-century organizations, being careful not to throw the baby out with the bathwater as is so often done in the creation of new concepts and models. We wanted to distil the archetypes of leaders that map onto people's real experience of how leaders act.

We wanted this new set of roles to cover the whole leadership territory, from team leader right up to the dizzy heights of chief executive officer (CEO). We wanted the roles to be well rounded and realistic, unlike the functionally divided competence sets which are often presented as definitive required behaviours, or the personality descriptions that are so often presented to leaders as a static picture of a non-developing, non-evolving person, acting independently from the environment. Our roles, instead, are more akin to the ideas that Meredith Belbin was proposing when he described the team roles that people tend to take, and emphasized the flexibility that we all have to shift role when we see it is necessary or desirable.

We also wanted to check through the change leadership literature to discover what successful leaders pay attention to. This is about their areas of focus, rather than their interpersonal behaviours. John Adair was the first to distinguish the three areas of focus for a competent leader. He named these as *team, task* and *individual*. This was a great starting point, but what other elements of organizational life need to be paid attention to, if you want to be a successful leader?

In the following paragraphs we take you through the highlights of the materials we used in our sifting and sorting exercise, to give you the experience of the journey we took to arrive at the five roles presented in this book.

So what are we not doing? We're not looking at character traits or personality types to predict a natural leadership style for any one person, we're not trying to pin leadership down to a set of competencies, we're not even saying that everyone should have a particular leadership style. What we are saying is that leaders need to take on different roles when it comes to leading change, and some of those roles may be more obvious and accessible to us than others.

WHAT DO SUCCESSFUL LEADERS DO?

Trait theory

Initial leadership studies in the 1940s attempted to attribute good leadership to the personal characteristics or traits of the leader. This was still a very prevalent belief during the early part of the 20th century when a lot of research was conducted into the sorts of traits that effective leaders had, and were assumed to have been born with. For example, Stogdill (1974) identified the following traits as critical to leaders:

- Adaptable to situations
- Alert to social environment
- Ambitious and achievement-orientated
- Assertive
- Cooperative
- Decisive
- Dependable
- Dominant (desire to influence others)
- Energetic (high activity level)
- Persistent
- Self-confident
- Tolerant of stress.

However, whilst many traits were spotted there was no real consensus on which set would make for an effective leader, or whether just having these traits would automatically guarantee success in leadership. This was less about 'what good leaders do', more about 'what good leaders are'.

Leadership attitudes and behaviours

Attitudes and behaviours of leaders became the focus of research from the 1950s onwards, with much of the attention being paid to developing dimensions for describing and measuring different types of behaviour and leadership orientation. Tannenbaum and Schmidt (1973) were interested in the authoritarian versus the democratic style. Blake and Mouton (1985) explored the task-focused leader versus the people-focused leader.

The authoritarian style was based on the notion that if management could structure and systematize the work and wield the necessary power, then the workers would act as if they were machines. However, the Human Relations School such as Herzberg and Maslow took the view that if you could engage workers by paying attention to how they felt and how they may wish to be motivated, ie by being more democratic and caring, then productivity would be increased.

Blake and Mouton developed this idea further by developing a model that illustrated that the best managers are concerned both about people and about production. They identified that a manager could display different levels of concern for the task and different levels of concern for people. This could range from low levels of concern for both task and people ('impoverished' management) through to high levels of concern for both task and people ('team' management), the latter being the most successful style.

Hersey and Blanchard (1988) went even further by looking at the level of competence and commitment of the team member and therefore suggesting that different styles of leadership would be more or less appropriate depending on the situation of the team member. This model became known at the 'situational leadership' model. They identified four styles known as directing, coaching, supporting and delegating.

Belbin's leadership roles

Anyone who has ever been on an away day with their team is very likely to have come across Meredith Belbin's team roles. These were identified by clustering behaviours, and labelling nine team roles that incorporate a combination of strengths and allowable weaknesses. Belbin described his team roles as 'a tendency to behave, contribute and interrelate with others in a particular way'. People who fill in a Belbin questionnaire receive a 'fingerprint' which indicates the two or three roles that they naturally inhabit.

The process allows people to explore the possibility of operating differently, should the environment require it. These nine roles are categorized into types in Table 4.1.

Table 4.1   Belbin type categories

Action-oriented roles	Shaper, Implementer, Completer Finisher
People-oriented roles	Coordinator, Teamworker, Resource Investigator
Cerebral roles	Plant, Monitor Evaluator, Specialist

John Adair's Action Centred Leadership

The advent of John Adair's simple model in the 1970s was a breath of fresh air into the leadership world. He was one of the first writers to demonstrate that leadership is a trainable skill, rather than an inborn ability. He also expanded the definition of management beyond task control and production to include decision making and communication activities. His Action Centred Leadership model is represented by three areas that managers need to pay attention to:

* achieving the task;

* managing the team or group;

* managing the individuals.

Management versus leadership

The 80s and 90s saw the emergence of notions of transformational, visionary leaders who instigated change, as opposed to the transactional managers who concerned themselves more with delegating pieces of work in return for good conditions, specific rewards and fair pay.

Bennis (1994) differentiated these roles quite clearly, by demonstrating that managers and leaders are very different animals (Table 4.2).

Table 4.2 Management versus leadership, Bennis (1994)

A manager	A leader
administers	innovates
is a copy	is an original
maintains	develops
focuses on systems and structure	focuses on people
relies on control	inspires trust
has a short-range view	has a long-range perspective
asks how and when	asks why
has his eye on the bottom line	has his eye on the horizon
imitates	originates
accepts the status quo	challenges the status quo
is the classic good soldier	is his own person
does things right	does the right thing

Kotter (1996) echoes the ideas of Bennis. He says '…we have raised a generation of very talented people to be managers, not leader/managers, and vision is not a component of effective management. The management equivalent to vision creation is planning.'

The six leadership styles that featured in Daniel Goleman's (2000) eye-catching article, 'Leadership that gets results', have influenced much leadership development activity over recent years, taking leaders beyond pure transactional management skills. Goleman discovered in his research that the use of each style has a unique effect on organizational climate over time, some positive and some negative. This in turn has a major influence on business results. The styles are known as coercive, authoritative, affiliative, democratic, coaching and pace-setting. Coercive and pace-setting are the two styles that have a depreciative effect on organizational climate if used continuously over time, and the authoritative (or visionary) style is the style that consistently has the most positive effects on organizational climate over time.

Principles and values

Stephen Covey's books have now become modern-day bibles for many people in organizations. Rather than focus on traits or competences, or what leaders pay attention to, he encourages people to develop underpinning principles that guide their actions. He emphasizes the need for positive solution-oriented thinking, good levels of listening, working with difference constructively, having a clear aim in life, continual learning and exploration, and maintaining a good balance between work and home.

The ideas behind authentic leadership move away from the study of style or behaviours of others, and instead focus on what's important to you as a leader, and who you are in relation to others. In his popular book *Authentic Leadership*, Bill George (2004) defines five key dimensions: understanding your purpose, practising solid values, leading with your heart, establishing connected relationships and demonstrating self-discipline. He says that being an authentic leader is about being true to yourself and your values – not presenting a false corporate image or trying to emulate the leadership style or characteristics of others.

A new kind of leader

Margaret Wheatley (1993) sees the ability of a leader to trust the organization's capacity to self-organize as the key to sustainable organizational success. Wheatley defines leadership as being about helping the organization to know itself, rather than about telling people what to do or giving them a vision. She says we need to think of the leader as a mirror who helps the organization know its own competencies, history and the business it's in. Wheatley says:

> If you're trying to create a healthy organization, one that can sustain itself over time, simply legislating and dictating behaviour and outcomes doesn't work at all... Leaders have to give up their belief that if they don't design the organization it won't structure itself... But we, as followers, have to give up our search for the perfect leader and give up the urge to turn it over to someone who will take care of it. We need to give all that up.

Leadership competences

We gathered together six sets of leadership competences gleaned from client organizations. Despite being derived via very different processes, these were remarkably similar. We were able to group the competences around seven areas encompassing both private and public sector organizations equally well.

Natural groupings of private and public sector leadership competences:

Focus on results
Strategic thinking
Influencing and partnering
Innovation and change
Customer/Stakeholder focus
Team building
Developing people

Conclusions about what leaders do

Having mapped out everything we knew about what good leaders do, we started to gather clusters of typical leadership roles which seemed to be related in terms of gesture, focus and emotionality (Table 4.3).

Table 4.3 Emerging clusters of leadership roles, Cameron and Green (2004)

Cluster one:	Confronter, problem spotter
Cluster two:	Energetic enabler, visionary, champion, motivator
Cluster three:	Driver, director, project manager
Cluster four:	Tester, innovator
Cluster five:	Guardian of the values, authentic influencer
Cluster six:	Listener, questioner, coach
Cluster seven:	Thinker, strategist, architect

WHAT DO SUCCESSFUL LEADERS PAY ATTENTION TO?

We complemented our research into what leaders do by reviewing the leadership literature for the answer to this question. We focused on literature covering the leadership of change, rather than looking at transactional management skills, because we see leadership roles as being primarily about making something happen that would not otherwise have happened.

This research began to fall naturally into the five key areas below:

- Discomfort – what's not working at the moment and who knows about this? Where is this organization hurting?

- Buy-in – how is it possible to harness the human resources and talent around the organization, and inspire, motivate and engage people?

- Connectivity – how do we ensure that the organization knows enough about itself and its purpose and competencies and is well connected enough to be able to self-organize and change in a healthy responsive way when it needs to?

- Projects – what needs to be done to manage key projects and ensure that all the necessary resources are acquired and that the projects are delivered on time, to budget and to the right quality?

- Design – what are the structural and process designs for the future?

Here's how each area was arrived at.

Discomfort

The need for people to feel discomfort appears to be a precursor for healthy change; the notion of tension or challenge crops up in much of the literature on organizational change. An important component of change, according to Kotter (1996), is the need to create a sense of urgency and to strongly challenge the prevailing wisdom. Other important writers on organizational change talk about the importance of a 'felt need' or a 'burning platform' as necessary conditions for change.

We found Heifetz's (1994) work insightful. Heifetz highlights what he calls the adaptive challenge and describes how leaders need to approach this. He says: 'Leadership is a razor's edge because one has to oversee a sustained period of social disequilibrium during which people confront the contradictions in their lives and communities and adjust their values and behaviour to accommodate new realities.'

Tichy and Devanna (1986) also see leaders as essentially agents for change, consciously and deliberately paying attention to what's not working and setting out to move the organization on. They identify one of the inner qualities of successful leaders as courage; identifying what needs to be changed and being able and willing to deal with resistance to the change.

Buy-in

It really helps a change process if the leaders are able to harness the human resources and talent around the organization, and to inspire, motivate and engage people to move the organization forward. Buy-in counts for a lot. However clear leaders might be about the strategy and the plan, personal charisma and an energetic and enthusiastic delivery go a long way to boost engagement.

Bass and Avolio (1990) identified three ways in which leaders achieve buy-in:

- sharing a vision and clear purpose in a way that commands interest and followership;

- focusing on individuals as they go through the journey of change, ensuring that their needs are met and that they are supported in their endeavours to develop;

- getting people excited and engaged, motivated and enthused in the change agenda.

The need for leaders to pay attention to this is echoed by many leading writers. Bennis and Nanus (1985) talk about creating attention through the vision and giving meaning through communication. Kotter (1996) and Kanter (1999) say that communicating a compelling vision together with empowering people to act and using other motivational strategies are essential areas of focus. Bennis (1996) describes this well. He says: 'Change leaders depend on being able to engage the hearts as well as the minds of the organization. This is greatly helped by an ability to empathize with what people at all levels are feeling; effective leaders put words to the formless feelings and deeply felt needs of others.'

Connectivity

Writers who apply complexity science to organizations, such as Margaret Wheatley, say that senior managers need to encourage self-organizing structures, rather than imposed ones. They believe that the best, most responsive solutions come from people who are constantly communicating with each other on the ground, rather than waiting for directives from above. In many organizations the world is moving too fast for people to wait for directives before responding to them in a pre-designed fashion. It is therefore extremely important for leaders to pay attention to connecting people in the organization and to helping them share and understand a common purpose.

Lipman-Blumen (2002) talks about 'connective' leaders who develop new ways of thinking and working with change. They confront and deal constructively with both interdependence (over-lapping visions, common problems) and diversity (distinctive character of individuals, groups and organizations). One of the preoccupations of change leaders when working with complex networks of stakeholders and partners is to ensure that all those involved make good connections with each other, and develop a sense of common purpose across boundaries, thus building commitment across a wide domain.

Senge (1993) also describes the role of the 'network leader' who is able to manage change by making connections:

> Senge makes the point that the really significant organizational challenges occur at the interfaces between project groups, functions and teams. Network leaders are people who work at these interfaces. They are guides, advisors, active helpers and accessors (helping groups of people to get resource from elsewhere); working in partnership with line leaders. They often have the insight to help local line leaders to move forward and make changes happen across the organization. (Cameron and Green, 2004)

Projects

It is sometimes easy to forget that actually the work has to be done, and someone has to do it. One of the major criticisms heard from front-line staff inside organizations is that leaders are long on rhetoric but short on delivery. Many organizations see this as somehow low-level or inferior work, or simply 'turning the handle'. However, when delivery is attended to well by leaders, organizations tend to experience success.

Heifetz (1994) emphasizes the need to maintain disciplined attention on business-as-usual, while Farkas and Wetlaufer (1996) stress the need for consistency and reliability, effective control systems and regular monitoring and evaluating. Binney and Williams (1995) also highlight the need for leaders to focus on operational credibility and to achieve some consistency of approach under pressure. Even Kotter, a big fan of vision, recognizes that an essential ingredient in any change plan is the existence of short-term wins.

Hind (1999) says that being solidly decisive and standing firm is vital, plus the ability to bring some order and control to the change process. Leadership of delivery is just as important as developing the vision in the first place.

Design

Bass and Avolio (1990) say that leaders need to stimulate their people intellectually. Innovative processes and organizational designs rely on bright people being able to come up with well-thought-through, workable strategies. Supply chains, customer loyalty programmes, global IT solutions, shared service centres, community development programmes... these things all need to be conceived and designed. Leaders therefore need to focus on eliciting new ideas and new ways of doing things.

Farkas and Wetlaufer (1996) identified that one of the important jobs of a CEO is to focus on strategy. This means devoting a great deal of their working time to ensuring the creation and implementation of a coherent long-term strategy.

THE FIVE LEADERSHIP ROLES

Our clustering exercise lasted several months. It involved clustering traits, competences, styles and attitudes together with the areas of focus; distilling key roles and then testing our ideas out extensively against leaders we knew to be successful, to see whether the roles fitted the real world. We then asked colleagues and clients to sense-check our ideas against successful leaders they know, and to measure themselves against the roles we had devised.

The final five role clusters are as they now appear in this book:

- Edgy Catalyser:
    - focuses on discomfort;
    - asks difficult questions, spots dysfunction and resistance, creates tension for change.

- Visionary Motivator:
    - focuses on buy-in;
    - articulates a compelling picture of the future, motivates and inspires people.

- Measured Connector
    - focuses on connectivity;
    - reinforces what's important and establishes a few simple rules, connects people and agendas.

- Tenacious Implementer
    - focuses on projects;
    - doggedly pursues the plan, holds people to account, leads by driving a project through to completion.

- Thoughtful Architect
    - focuses on design;
    - is principal architect and designer of the strategies, crafts seemingly disparate ideas into a way forward, scans the environment, sees what's happening in the environment and creates an organizing framework.

Part 2

Understanding the five roles

5

The Edgy Catalyser

THE EDGY CATALYSER ROLE IN A NUTSHELL

'This is a serious problem. Can't you get some traction on this?'

- Asks the difficult, penetrating questions.
- Spots dysfunction and resistance.
- Creates discomfort and unease when things aren't improving.
- Focuses on 'discomfort'.

The Edgy Catalyser focuses on creating tension between what is and what could or should be, and sees the process of facing uncomfortable truths as a precursor to healthy change.

Research findings

- Best used in small doses.
- Selected by the leaders in our survey as the least attractive role model.
- Not a popular choice as a boss.
- Positively correlated with the Tenacious Implementer role.
- Eight per cent of the leaders in our survey said this was their natural leadership role.
- Thirty per cent of the leaders in our survey named this role as the hardest to adopt.
- Thoughtful Architects tend to find the Edgy Catalyser role particularly difficult to access.
- Useful role during restructuring process, in times of crisis or when facing well-defined change.

ALL ABOUT THE EDGY CATALYSER ROLE

The Edgy Catalyser is the leader who smells a rat and points at it. This person is an intelligent agitator who spots real problems, especially if they are hard to face, and adds the right amount of tension and pressure to ensure that the difficulty is addressed. This process is likely to feel quite uncomfortable for those involved, but the secret of the Edgy Catalyser is that he or she doesn't get stressed out by conflict; in fact this type of leader is happier when there is discomfort and a need for action in the air.

In this role, the leader has the uncanny ability to ask just the right penetrating question, point the finger at one part of the organization, or question the accepted wisdom of the business in order to get people to see that things might need to change. The Edgy Catalyser can illuminate tensions and conflicts which, if focused on and worked through, will lead to renewal. In times of change these leaders will spot resistance, spot dysfunction, spot where the fires need to be lit and blow on the glowing embers. They are happy to be seen as the troubleshooters, troublemakers or catalysts for change.

Edgy Catalysers are not disconnected from the business goals. In fact, their skill is to hold the strategic direction and organizational purpose in their minds, and see clearly where the structure, the systems, the infrastructure or the people are failing. They can take a step back or knock the machine in the right place with a hammer to illustrate its weak points. But they don't just focus on the negatives; they may also focus very assertively on what's going right, and demand the same performance or outcomes from the rest of the organization.

These people are not intimidated by politics, but are clever enough to respect its power. They can assimilate and respect the prevailing vision and values, and point out, for example, where executives are failing to role-model agreed values, or where expensive IT systems are falling short of expectations and costing too much effort in workarounds, or where one team is achieving great results while others appear to struggle. They are courageous enough to tackle the difficult stuff that's hard to mention. They might confront people or teams with their unhelpful behaviours if people-focused, or with their disappointing results or ailing processes if task-focused. They tend to see things from a systemic point of view, having an awareness of what's going on beneath the surface, and can highlight the log-jams, and with minimal intervention can alter the flow of things by enabling or diverting attention, energy or resources.

A typical example of an Edgy Catalyser is a new leader who arrives in an organization and sees everything with fresh eyes, drawing everyone's attention to what's not right, or what's surprising or what compares badly to other organizations. Some people find this type of leadership irritating and hard to deal with, while others find it exhilarating. It needs to be done intelligently and with respect, but nonetheless there will be tension around. People with cross-organizational leadership roles such as performance directors, quality managers, corporate social responsibility managers and health & safety managers often need to carry out an Edgy Catalyser Role, alerting people to issues and being a thorn in people's sides until they take action.

Susan Scott's book *Fierce Conversations* points out that this type of boldness and courage is the only way to avoid the creeping death of *The Corporate Nod*. This is the familiar scenario in which the boss presents the obviously flawed plan, but no one is brave enough to point out the problem. The only way to combat *The Corporate Nod* is boldness – as long as you are prepared to pay the price for being authentically you. Scott gives the example of a manager who enters his boss's office with a bucket of sand and pours it on the floor, saying 'I just figured I'd make it easier for you to bury your head in the sand on the topic I keep bringing up and you keep avoiding.' The ensuing conversation was difficult, but life-changing. Scott also says 'the truth will set you free – but first it will thoroughly irritate you'. Edgy Catalysers definitely have to court the anger of others by having a potent mix of courage and good judgement and a relatively thick skin.

HEART AND SOUL OF THE EDGY CATALYSER ROLE

The Edgy Catalyser cares deeply about getting things right. Their very presence can be a huge motivating factor in any team, even though they may feel like a thorn in the organization's side at times. They can appear very tough-minded and blunt, but this is connected to their overriding commitment to saying it as it is and pointing out the issues. They cannot sit idly by because they care so much about the quality of the end result.

They are courageous people and value this trait in others. They are not afraid to speak their mind. As such they naturally adopt a questioning approach and don't suffer fools gladly. However, they are equally liable to spot what's good in organizations, although they value the tension that this can create with those who aren't performing up to scratch yet.

An Edgy Catalyser displays honesty and integrity which can be quite uncompromising and often unequivocal. Respect is gained through tough engagement not social niceties. Edgy Catalysers value the ability to push boundaries (in terms of systems, structures, behaviours, etc), ruffle feathers and face conflict as a means to achieving agreed goals.

THE EDGY CATALYSER'S INNER EXPERIENCE

What they're thinking

Edgy Catalysers have a tendency to detach themselves from a situation and look at it objectively. They can quickly analyse what's not working, and what needs to be challenged. Then they assess what to do next by judging people's initial responses. Empathy does not feature in the Edgy Catalyser's natural toolkit. In fact, shutting out empathy enables this type of leader to make a good logical case and to assess situations and people. Empathy, however, will definitely be required to work out how much pressure, or tension, to use to raise the difficult issues to the surface. The Edgy Catalyser may have to calibrate him or herself, because overdoing the tension or pressure can be counterproductive.

How they're feeling

Natural Edgy Catalysers feel alive when there is conflict in the air. They tend to like robust argument, and enjoy working with people who stand up for themselves, although they don't always let people know this. On a bad day they might meet conflict with yet more conflict, which can look like annoyance or irritation, which may have the unintended effect of causing their more empathic colleagues to back off or back down.

Some Edgy Catalysers have developed successful ways of dealing with conflict. This usually involves being courageous, and having faith that if a conflict is entered into respectfully it will lead to a positive outcome. They use the facts to argue a point and listen to the counter-arguments. Mature Edgy Catalysts are also able to face anger or fear in others with a determined steadiness.

Less mature Edgy Catalysers struggle with their own feelings of anger and fear, especially if they are openly challenged, and may lose control through what Daniel Goleman (1998) calls an 'amygdala highjack'. This is more widely known as 'losing it' and can feature table banging, swearing and other behaviours that diminish themselves and others. This is when the Edgy Catalyser can become a liability to the organization. It may be useful for these leaders to investigate the triggers for angry episodes and develop some new ways of thinking when those triggers are around. Sometimes leaders with these patterns of behaviour benefit from external professional support such as coaching, counselling or mentoring.

THE EDGY CATALYSER'S OUTER PRESENTATION

Posture

Natural Edgy Catalysers very often have a straight back, fidgety feet or hands, an inability to sit still for long periods, a roving eye; always scanning the area for people or things, very often sitting forward in their seats. They look you in the eye only when they need to and will signal boredom very quickly, particularly if someone else is talking too long and getting off the point.

Upsides

Natural Edgy Catalysers are really good in a crisis; they thrive in such conditions. They are comfortable with upset and controversy, and have no worries about being liked or accepted. In fact, being liked and accepted would cause them great concern! These people have incredible energy for noticing the things that matter, arguing the point, having the difficult conversations and getting people to focus on the right things.

Downsides

Because of their incredible energy, bordering on obsession, they might take too much on, putting undue pressure on themselves (which they can sometimes handle) and on others (who might not be able to handle it). Their inability to rest on their laurels just for a moment and enjoy a bit of success or completion can lead to them becoming workaholics.

They are continually haunted by the possibility that things are not good enough, and imperfection, stupidity and failure is only a step away. This means that they are exhausting people to work for and probably to live with. They might like to consider celebrating success, and being less critical of themselves.

Natural Edgy Catalysers often find it difficult to calibrate their leadership approach in terms of directness and level of open criticism. Some organizational contexts need a lot of edge and tension, while others need more appreciation and support. Edgy Catalysers may not be good at noticing when the context has changed, and they can now back off or turn the volume down.

What they're not

The Edgy Catalyser is not a bully, or an over-controlling manager. This role involves much more attention to the facts and a more authentic, up-front approach to discussing 'what is' than a bully or a control freak would be able to tolerate. The Edgy Catalyser can be questioned and challenged, whereas the bully avoids challenge by ignoring or dismissing other people's points of view in an aggressive way. The over-controlling manager simply wants things done his or her way and will not discuss options. Neither is the Edgy Catalyser a 'naysayer' who opposes progress and clings to a set of rigid rules.

ORGANIZATIONAL ASPECTS OF THE EDGY CATALYSER ROLE

Every organizational environment or 'culture' is uniquely different and the Edgy Catalyser must adapt a little to the prevailing culture to be successful.

The Edgy Catalyser needs to be able to conform just enough to keep to the organizational ground-rules without losing the ability to sustain a conflictual stance, and needs to avoid the very real possibility of being 'spat out' of the organization for being too controversial and in some way unacceptable.

In a mechanistic organization, eg a manufacturing company or an IT department, the Edgy Catalyser needs to get the facts right and plan carefully when to tackle the issue and with whom. In this type of organization, people believe that change will work best if it is well executed and controlled and managed by the right people in the right roles. The Edgy Catalyser has to fit in with this to some extent and is more likely to be successful in helping change to happen if the aim is to get people to update the plan and tune the structure rather than throw everything up in the air and start again. The latter may create so much resistance that the result is unmanageable.

In a political organization the Edgy Catalyser needs to pay attention to coalitions and allegiances and to individual agendas. Embarrassing individuals in front of their staff teams is not a good idea, and neither is giving even minor surprises at a formal meeting. If the Edgy Catalyser notices a big problem, it's best if the most powerful people involved in the issue are 'on-side' first, before the subject is opened up for wider discussion.

In a more messy and fluid organization change happens through emergence rather than via a rational planning process. This means that constant collaboration and competition go on all around the organization, and because of a strong sense of purpose and strong connections within the organization, change happens in a more spontaneous, less controlled way. This means that the Edgy Catalyser will need to find the group of people for whom the issue is also a concern to unlock the energy to solve the problem. For instance, in a decentralized oil company that we worked with, there was a big problem with management information. This was most strongly felt in one division, where recent errors in information analysis had resulted in some unpleasant and embarrassing legal complications. The Edgy Catalyser performance director focused her attention on this division, giving them one month to find a solution, and offering central resources to help them do so. This resulted in a solution that was then applied successfully to all divisions.

In adaptive organizations people believe that when the environment changes, the organization must carefully design its response through participation and involvement. In this environment the Edgy Catalyser may spot a problem such as a lack of focus on financial targets. This needs to be communicated to key teams by connecting it to a real change in the environment that necessitates internal change, eg 'the external auditors are now looking for more evidence that we do this', or 'customers now require to see our accounting processes'. This may seem rather complicated, but is usually worth the effort, because in this type of culture the existence of an external driver is vital.

EXAMPLES OF EDGY CATALYSERS

Sir Alan Sugar, the UK-born entrepreneur and one-time football magnate, is a good example of a natural Edgy Catalyser. He has been hugely successful in the electronics industry, and is now a self-styled management guru having starred in the BBC TV series _The Apprentice_. In this programme he selects one recruit from a batch of young hopefuls by observing how well they do in a series of highly challenging team tasks. Sir Alan is highly admired for his bluntness. He advertises himself as tough and abrasive and advocates decisive action, evidenced by him urging the team leaders in the programme to 'forget the nicey nicey stuff'.

He is oozing with raw commercial energy, and like many Edgy Catalysers is motivated entirely by commercial success. Apparently he used to get up at 6 am when he was a teenager to boil beetroots for a local greengrocer for cash.

His most public catalytic action was to sack the extremely popular manager of Tottenham Hotspur Football Club, Terry Venables. He was pilloried by the press and fans, and it was a very isolating time for him. 'I felt as though I'd killed Bambi', he said rather poignantly, but he stuck with the decision and rode the storm, typical of the Edgy Catalyser.

Mainland Europe has its fair share of Edgy Catalysers too. Siemens' ex-CEO Klaus Kleinfeld is a hard-hitting, highly successful and totally committed industrialist. He brought stunning commercial success to Siemens, boosting profits by an astonishing 35 per cent within two years of his arrival and increasing the share price by 40 per cent. He achieved this through gritty determination, a degree of isolation from his colleagues, and an enormous will to challenge the whole way in which German industry works, including fundamental labour laws. He courted conflict right from the start.

At the personal level he was demanding, challenging and uncomfortably direct. When asked about his management style he said, 'We commit to something and we deliver. That is the culture we want to form.' Behind the scenes he was pushy and insistent, known for his unstoppable energy and his persistent phone calls. 'If you turn off your phone, he calls your wife', said one manager.

Although loved by the worldwide financial press, he was heavily criticized by the unions over his harsh 'Anglo-American' leadership style, and the German media was full of venom when the elite senior management team at Siemens awarded themselves a large pay rise, while countless workers were being made redundant. It didn't help Kleinfeld's case when he very publicly dropped a journalist's phone into a glass of water, saying it wasn't the right brand. This act was described by his more sympathetic colleagues as 'high jinks' but you can't help wondering whether he took his confrontational style too far.

Kleinfeld elected to stand down from the CEO role in April 2007, leaving the company after just three years there. He was evidently lacking board support and his resignation was accepted despite his impressive commercial record. The named cause of lack of support from his colleagues on the board was the consternation regarding several allegations of bribery within the Siemens ranks, although this was never linked to Kleinfeld himself. Some say that the board failed to support Kleinfeld because some of his wider challenges to the German way of working were too much too fast, and they just didn't have the stomach for it.

One CEO in a large international manufacturing business used the Edgy Catalyser role to excellent effect, and in a way that was respectful of others. When she joined the company as CEO, one of the many production plants had just been through a huge change programme, involving a significant investment. The old plant had been closed down and hundreds of people had been made redundant. The new plant had opened on time, but three months on was still suffering from endless teething problems, and customers were starting to go elsewhere. There had been such high hopes for this new site, and now it appeared to be seriously under-delivering.

She started asking questions of those connected with the site, but didn't get much more than 'wait and see', 'it's OK, it's under control' and 'it's early days'. She felt fobbed off, but gave it another two months, understanding that these things do take time. Then she began to get a little impatient. She announced that she would be visiting the site and was keen to speak to everyone involved. She let everyone know that this site was failing in her eyes and that she needed to know the exact situation and what would be done about the loss of business and company profile, insisting that she wanted the truth, and that this situation needed to be clarified and dealt with.

This piece of Edgy Catalyser leadership caused the local management team involved to face reality in a very uncomfortable way. As a result, they decided to reopen the old site to ensure that customer orders continued to be fulfilled while they sorted out the new plant. This wouldn't have happened without pressure from the top as it involved people coming to terms with some harsh realities, dealing with errors of judgement and making a really uncomfortable u-turn by having to go back to people who had been made redundant a year earlier and asking them to come back to work.

Alex Ferguson, manager of Manchester United for over two decades, also uses the Edgy Catalyser role well. When he first arrived at Manchester United he called all the players together. The situation at the club was dire; the crowds had dropped below 40,000 and the team was very near the bottom of the league. Everyone was dispirited and there was discontent. Norman Whiteside, the former midfielder, said: 'It was not so much what he said, as the tone of his voice. We knew he meant business.' Part of what was wrong was the drinking culture in the club. He is quoted as saying 'I'm running a football club, not a drinking club'. When his warnings went unheeded he simply got rid of the worst offenders. Bryan Robson, the club captain and English international, described Ferguson's style when he said: 'He made it clear what he wanted, so you either changed or you carried on what you were doing. Inevitably, if anyone ignored him he would move them on.'

Vladimir Putin, President of Russia, also shows signs of Edgy Catalyser leadership. He was at a press conference with George Bush in 2006, defending his country's democratic record. Referring to Bush's notion of Iraq's 'democratization', Putin said: 'We certainly would not want to have the same kind of democracy as they have in Iraq, I will tell you quite honestly.' He was blunt and to the point. *The Independent* newspaper described him beautifully. 'His cold smile and athletic stride convey a sense of energy and authority. It is not an accidental impression.' A survey of a representative sample of 1,500 Russians named the president's strong points as decisiveness, ability to pursue goals, toughness, calm in the face of provocation, and self-confidence.

Senator Hilary Clinton, wife of former president Bill Clinton and presidential candidate, was described by Bill as conveying '... a sense of strength and self-possession I had rarely seen in anyone, man or woman'. Political psychologist Aubrey Immelman describes her more candidly, declaring: 'In short, what we have in Candidate Clinton is a controlling, competitive, somewhat disagreeable individual with little inclination for kindness, yet highly disciplined and dedicated, if somewhat closed-minded and inflexible.' Hilary appears to use the Edgy Catalyser role. She is a deep thinker who can spot things which are wrong and focus people's attention on an issue, diverting energy and enthusiasm to ensure that something is done.

Bill Gates, founder and chairman of Microsoft, has legendary Edgy Catalyser qualities. His CEO Steve Ballmer recounts why it is so important to be prepared – very prepared – before a meeting with Gates. Gates' drive and intelligence and will to win mean that any meeting with him can be like a final exam, with Gates picking holes in any plans or ideas that don't stack up. Others describe him as demanding, confrontational, uncompromising and explosive.

6

The Visionary Motivator

THE VISIONARY MOTIVATOR ROLE IN A NUTSHELL

'Let's all move towards a brighter future.'

- Articulates a compelling picture of the future.

- Energizes groups of people and engages them.

- Holds the vision long enough and strong enough for others to step into.

- Focuses on the 'buy-in'.

Visionary Motivators focus on harnessing the human resources and talent around the organization. They inspire, motivate and engage people in the organization's future by employing emotionally charged language and using metaphor to create a vibrant and collective sense of potential.

Research findings

- The role most widely used by effective leaders.
- Selected by the leaders in our survey as the most attractive role model (47%).
- A popular choice as a boss.
- Most people want more of it in organizational life.
- Twenty-six per cent of the leaders in our survey said this was their natural leadership role.
- Seventeen per cent of the leaders in our survey named this role as the hardest to adopt.
- Tenacious Implementers find this role particularly difficult to access.
- Useful role during situations that require growth, or to combat low morale, or when change is complex and far-reaching.

ALL ABOUT THE VISIONARY MOTIVATOR ROLE

The Visionary Motivator articulates a compelling picture of the future and enlists others in the journey. They give purpose to people in their day-to-day roles. The Visionary Motivator begins by suggesting a possible future and rapidly engages others in this. The vision itself tends to be a reflection of followers' needs and wishes, and creates interest and excitement without being prescriptive or narrow.

These leaders are very effective motivators and enablers. They connect with people quickly and easily, and their desire to move forward towards achieving things for everyone is infectious, whilst at the same time they are able to use their interpersonal skills to affirm, encourage and excite colleagues and followers. They hold the vision long enough and strong enough for others to step into it. In that sense they can be described as motivational coaches, working with individuals to help them understand the future and see a clear part for themselves in it.

An important element of the Visionary Motivator's natural approach is that they role-model what it's like to be motivated and inspired. They are energetic and relentlessly upbeat, and have the vitality and the passion to draw people along in their wake. They have clarity of purpose and the dynamism to go with it. The Visionary Motivator wins the respect and trust of followers by inviting them to believe that they can achieve more than they ever thought possible.

Visionary Motivators can also take the role of the salesperson, quickly marshalling the relevant facts to produce an on-the-spot compelling 'business case' for change. They will find the right levers, pull the right strings, push the right buttons. They may point out what the future will bring, talk about how it will feel to get there, spot and highlight the environmental trends and encourage, coax, cajole and coach people towards a brighter future.

Visionary Motivators usually have credibility within the leadership domain. It's unlikely that a leader who is inexperienced in a particular field could act as a Visionary Motivator and be successful with experienced followers. It would be hard for people to give credence to their ability to establish a compelling vision.

Richard Branson is a good example of someone who uses the Visionary Motivator role when he can. He is very good at promoting himself and his brand, and is full of big, bold ideas and convincing grand plans. He is tirelessly energetic and always full of stories of success. However, when asked for details on failures or pitfalls he has been quoted as saying he doesn't really remember his mistakes, and certainly doesn't dwell on them. This is another important dimension to the Visionary Motivator; they can be relied upon to be positive, but they are not often reflective.

HEART AND SOUL OF THE VISIONARY MOTIVATOR ROLE

Visionary Motivators bring energy to organizational life that is often lacking. They are willing to put themselves forward, possibly to be laughed at or pilloried, but they truly value the type of leadership that sets direction, gets buy-in and goes for it.

They enjoy innovative ideas that illuminate a better future, and enjoy talking about their ideas in a new and engaging way. They take a keen interest in language, particularly use of words, and get inspired by what other people say. They would like to live in a better world and they would like others to join them there, and their belief can shine through organizations like a beacon in the darkness. They will do what they can to enable the people and processes to move in the right direction, short of actually doing it themselves.

They value people with enthusiasm and a positive approach. They value optimism, perhaps occasionally over realism. They like proactivity, and prefer this to a slower, more measured approach.

THE VISIONARY MOTIVATOR'S INNER EXPERIENCE

What they're thinking

Visionary Motivators think that the glass is half full. They think positively and proactively about the future. They are optimistic and future-focused. They see opportunities and possible solutions rather than problems and want everyone to be part of the solution, not part of the problem. They are usually busy thinking how they can do something differently, not why it won't work. They are also anxious to get on with things. The power of positive thought will help propel them forward.

How they're feeling

They're feeling good. They have a real sense of direction and generally feel quite buoyant. They see the upside in most things and most people. Sometimes they just can't see what other people's problem is – they're happy to just see and feel the upside of everything.

The only thing that might lower their spirits is other people's pessimism or inertia. Rolling eyes or blank stares don't go down very well with Visionary Motivators.

THE VISIONARY MOTIVATOR'S OUTER PRESENTATION

Posture

They have a spring in their step and often wear a smile. They have a presence that's hard to ignore. They like to keep moving and are quite expressive in their bodily movements. They can often get closer physically than some people prefer, perhaps touching others on the arm or shoulders when in conversation, as an expression of warmth or acceptance.

Upsides

The Visionary Motivator will tend to kick-start things and get the show on the road. They can lift people's spirits and create a 'can do' atmosphere in which others feel that anything is possible and the vision can actually be achieved. There's a real sense of maximizing people's potential and of collective enthusiasm, energy and dynamism that can be infectious.

Downsides

Being with the Visionary Motivator can be exhausting! The boundless energy and need to keep moving forward can take its toll and followers can begin to lose momentum. When leaders accentuate the positive all the time, some people can become cynical. Change isn't always felt as positive and some people like to take stock of the situation, or slow down. Others want to protect some of the current ways of doing things. And yet more might like to express their anger and frustration about the way the changes are going, which the Visionary Motivator doesn't particularly like to hear and may get irritated with, thus switching people off even more.

There is sometimes a tendency for the Visionary Motivator to miss important details, or worse, to move onto the next enthusiasm before the current project has been fully understood or completed.

What they're not

Visionary Motivators are not over-parental characters who take care of things for people. Nether are they actors or entertainers who simply make people laugh, or take their mind off work for an hour or so. Neither are they liars or fantasists. What they say has at least a modicum of substance, and leads to an energetic response from people.

ORGANIZATIONAL ASPECTS OF THE VISIONARY MOTIVATOR ROLE

Every organizational environment or 'culture' is uniquely different and the Visionary Motivator must adapt a little to the culture if he or she is to be successful.

How can the Visionary Motivator adapt his or her style? They are most interested in galvanizing and energizing people to move forward in a particular direction. They therefore may have some difficulties when in an overly mechanistic or political environment. Likewise if the direction is unclear or if environmental shifts dictate the direction they may become less certain about adopting their role.

In a mechanistic organization the Visionary Motivator will probably have to downplay the overly passionate part of their nature. In some ways they may need to appear like the Tenacious Implementer but perhaps with more outwardly expressed drive, dedication and conscientiousness.

There are two key things for the Visionary Motivator to hold in mind in a mechanistic setting. The first is to ensure that the vision is firmly connected into the strategies, objectives and project plans. There is no room for an 'airy fairy' vision that is disconnected from the everyday workings of the organization. And secondly, their motivational techniques must be aligned and attuned to the mechanistic culture. Exaggerated positivism is unlikely to succeed, whereas motivational strategies tied into the systems and structures of the organization will be welcomed. Reward systems, performance coaching and performance management would be typical techniques within this culture.

In a political organization, the Visionary Motivator needs to be aware that just being positive and having a clear direction won't necessarily win over everyone's heart and mind. A political culture involves the exercising of different forms of power, with the allocation of resources relating to shifting interests. This requires the Visionary Motivator to be focused on getting close to the different stakeholder groups and being able to exert impact and influence according to both the explicit and implicit needs and wants of these groups. An understanding of stakeholder management together with a sound working knowledge of motivational theory and practice will be required.

In messy and fluid cultures the Visionary Motivator won't always have the clarity and certainty of direction that they may have in other arenas. So rather than concentrate on a particular vision they may have to focus on generating a degree of ongoing confidence in the change, or in a broader sense of purpose... wherever it might lead. The key will be to get people energized and mobilized – perhaps by creating a sense of urgency in the present or perhaps by talk of a future 'promised land'. Getting people together to buy into the change when the future is uncertain requires the Visionary Motivator to put some stakes in the ground, indicate broad direction and exude the confidence of someone who knows that the process will work and the journey be worthwhile. Helping people generate options is important.

One of the attributes of the Visionary Motivator is the ability to turn problems into opportunities; reframe events positively and see the bright side of life. So in an adaptive culture where the organization needs to have the capability to react effectively and proactively to changes they are a great asset. When looking at a SWOT analysis (strengths and weaknesses of the organization, opportunities and threats from the environment) the Visionary Motivator will be able to see ways of exploiting the organizational strengths and environmental opportunities and ways to mitigate the organizational weaknesses and environmental threats. They'll be able to reframe things positively, whatever is on the horizon, and they'll help people understand the 'what if…' scenarios.

EXAMPLES OF VISIONARY MOTIVATORS

Tony Blair, former UK prime minister, is a good example of a Visionary Motivator. If you read his speeches, you will notice that he constantly urges people to work towards a better future. As Bashir Goth wrote in the *Washington Post* of Blair's early years in power:

> Tony Blair came into power like a hero on a galloping stallion, young and zealous to change the Labour Party and the world. He was a man shedding his youthful socialist ideals and coming to grips with Thatcherite economic realities. He clicked with his equally media savvy and more politically suave counterpart in the White House, Bill Clinton. Riding on the wave of New Labour, Blair transformed the UK into one of the most robust economies in Europe, and struck a partnership with Clinton in following the Third Way philosophy. He embraced globalization with full faith and ushered in the 21st century with grand dreams, and has through his charisma won the 2012 Olympic Games to be hosted in London.

In Alastair Campbell's diary *The Blair Years*, Campbell (Tony Blair's former press secretary) recounts the process whereby Tony Blair began to engage potential voters in his ideas, and in New Labour:

> Tony felt he was on to something with the stakeholder economy idea. It was a way of conveying that the economy is about more than money and jobs, it was also about what sort of country we wanted to be. It worked perfectly in tandem with One Nation. It was also a washing line from which to hang all the different parts of economic policy... Tony said we now needed two things, the sense of the team and main players working in harmony, and the feeling that the Tories were no longer making the economy improve.

This was how the New Labour vision began to emerge; through taking words and phrases and testing them out for resonance with groups of people, and using them to group policies or activities together. This is typical of a Visionary Motivator, as they work best when they're putting motivating ideas together; others can work up the detail.

A key attribute of the Visionary Motivator is his or her ability to truly inspire people. William Shirer says of Mahatma Gandhi, another Visionary Motivator, 'I count the days with Gandhi the most fruitful of my life. No other experience was as inspiring and as meaningful and as lasting. No other so shook me out of the rut of banal existence and opened my ordinary mind and spirit.'

We worked with a Visionary Motivator who was a chief executive unexpectedly appointed from the management team after the abrupt removal of the previous, rather autocratic, CEO. The organization was going through a considerable financial crisis due to the previous CEO's style. He had ignored all objections to his expansionist plans and his risky diversification strategy. The new CEO, now 55, had joined the company at 16 and had worked nowhere else, working himself up from the most junior position through branch manager, regional manager and various other roles. Latterly he was in charge of creating new business units and organizing acquisitions, which he had done successfully.

The new CEO had two big advantages in this situation. He had credibility and he had an excellent interpersonal style which meant he could get close to people quickly. He immediately told people about the nature of the company crisis – unlike the previous CEO who chose to ignore it – and created a sense of urgency and belief in a possible future together. His network of contacts reached throughout the organization and he was able to appeal to their values by laying on the line that the company itself, with its proud traditions, was likely to go under. The future was uncertain, and yet he was able to exude the confidence to get people to rally round, holding onto the traditions as a lifebelt.

This leader had a strong self-belief, but he also had immense belief in the managers and staff and he made that very clear in communication after communication. These were most often face-to-face events, in both large and small groups. He also worked hard on rebuilding the fragmented management team by focusing in on individual and collective motivations. He was thus able to form a guiding coalition to develop a new strategy together with a new vision and he successfully achieved world-class customer service through the team within two years.

We worked with another Visionary Motivator in a turnaround situation in the manufacturing industry. He was promoted to MD of a £1 billion business with steadily declining market and profit levels. He arrived with credibility in the specific business area, and he had the advantage of an arresting physical presence; when he entered the room you knew about it. He had a booming voice, was over six feet tall, and he had a tendency to really look you in the eye and make you feel the sole focus of his attention.

He was keen to tour round all the different sites, explaining his 10-point plan to the front-line workers, who were disarmed by his frankness about the problems that the business was facing and his upbeat affirmation of them as important people. They soon became committed to working hard for him personally. He also set about repairing broken relationships with key suppliers, and as a result reversed the stagnant, negative relationships that were there when he arrived.

He decided to raise prices to reflect the prevailing market conditions and sent his sales force out to put this to customers. Many disagreed with this decision, but in the end, the move enabled the company to make a great deal of money that was subsequently invested in new equipment and essential refurbishments.

He left after nearly three years, having changed the culture and the bottom line dramatically. Many didn't like being told what to do, but they had to admit that this leader was able to win over the hearts and minds of the majority, to the benefit of the whole business.

Anita Roddick, the founder of the Body Shop, who died in 2007, epitomizes the visionary entrepreneurs of the last half of the 20th century. *The Scotsman* newspaper remembered her, stating: 'With her charismatic personality, Roddick became an accepted face of business and proved a visionary in the boardroom and in political matters. She was a tireless and articulate campaigner on moral and social issues: subjects on which she spoke with a resounding vehemence.' Interestingly her autobiography was entitled *Body and Soul*. Ralph Nader described her as 'a glorious combination of character and personality who had her priorities high and wide enough to ask the most fundamental questions of big business and answer them by her deeds and her words'.

Ronald Reagan, former US president, was a very different personality with very different politics and yet had many behaviours characteristic of the Visionary Motivator too. Gil Troy in his book *Morning in America: How Ronald Reagan Invented the 1980s* describes Reagan as friendly, and optimistic, a visionary, 'the Moses of the conservative revolution'. Joseph Wood, the freelance writer and journalist, summarizes Reagan thus:

> Reagan is considered by most Americans to be the most popular figure in American politics in our lifetime. 'The Great Communicator' was not only great at telling one-liners, spinning tales, and charmingly timing his perfectly punched phrases. He had great ideas behind his finely crafted words... He was a great man of letters as well as public speaking... He was an optimistic soul. He made Americans feel optimistically about the future, as well as the present.

In his own words Reagan sums up his Visionary Motivator stance:

> I won a nickname, 'The Great Communicator', but I never thought it was my style or the words I used that made a difference: it was the content. I wasn't a great communicator, but I communicated great things, and they didn't spring full bloom from my brow, they came from the heart of a great nation, from our experience, our wisdom, and our belief in principles that have guided us for two centuries. They called it the Reagan revolution. Well, I'll accept that, but for me it always seemed more like the great rediscovery, a rediscovery of our values and our common sense.

Howard Schultz, the recently reappointed CEO of Starbucks, is an interesting leader, combining many different roles, as many really excellent leaders do. However, his most obvious and most impressive role is the Visionary Motivator role. In his autobiography, *Pour Your Heart Into It*, he illustrates this beautifully by saying:

> Again and again, I've had to use every ounce of perseverance and persuasion I can summon to make things happen. Life is a series of near misses. But a lot of what we subscribe to is not luck at all. It's seizing the day and accepting responsibility for your future. It's seeing what other people don't see and pursuing that vision no matter who tells you not

> to. ... when you really believe – in yourself, in your dream – you just have to do everything you possibly can to take control and make your vision a reality.

These are fine words, but it does seem to be the case for Schultz. In 1982 he joined Starbucks as director of marketing, and worked hard to persuade the traditional coffee-bean store to start selling cups of coffee in their stores. He resigned in frustration at their resistance, experimented himself, and came back and bought the company a year later. Starbucks then expanded throughout the 90s, under his inspiring leadership. Schultz said that he wanted to build a 'company with soul'. He did just this. He was amongst the first employers in the United States to offer comprehensive health coverage and an employee stock-option plan. His vision was real to him, and he focused on engaging others in making it happen.

More recently, there have been problems at Starbucks; falling share prices due to an overtly expansionist approach which diluted the value of the 'Starbucks experience'. Stiff competition from cheaper alternatives like McDonalds didn't help either. Schultz's leaked in-company memo, written in February 2007 to a boardroom colleague, shows both his disappointment and his passion. Here's a short quote as he vents his frustrations about the way the whole feel of the stores has changed in recent years:

> Stores... no longer have the soul of the past, and reflect a chain of stores versus the warm feeling of a neighborhood store. Some people even call our stores sterile, cookie cutter, no longer reflecting the passion our partners feel about our coffee. In fact, I am not sure people today even know we are roasting coffee. You certainly can't get the message from being in our stores... some stores don't even have coffee grinders...

It seems that Schultz still has the Visionary Motivator's energy to get Starbucks out of the doldrums.

James Dyson is best known for being a great entrepreneur. He persevered in his desire to produce a bagless vacuum cleaner by building over five thousand prototypes before he got it right. He now has a worldwide reputation for innovative design and 1,300 employees, a £190 million turnover and a personal fortune estimated to be over £500m.

Dyson clearly has much of the Tenacious Implementer about him, often described as determined and stubborn. However, when you hear him speak about engineering, business and innovation, the overriding impression is a Visionary Motivator who is both passionate and optimistic. He says:

> The key to success is failure, I would guess. Not other people's failure, but how you respond to failure yourself. Everyone gets knocked back, no one rises smoothly to the top without hindrance. The ones who succeed are those who say, right, let's give it another go. Who cares what others think? I believe in what I am doing. I will never give up. Success is made of 99 per cent failure. You galvanize yourself and you keep going, as a full optimist... Hope is the most important element in success... I learned that the moment you want to slow down is the moment you should accelerate. In long distance running, you go through a pain barrier. The same thing happens in research and development projects, or in starting any business. There's a terrible moment when failure is staring you in the face. And actually if you persevere a bit longer you'll start to climb out of it.

7

The Measured Connector

THE MEASURED CONNECTOR ROLE IN A NUTSHELL

'Get together and take time to focus on this.'

- Reinforces what's important and establishes a few simple rules.

- Calmly influences complex change activity through focused reassurance.

- Connects people and agendas.

- Focuses on 'connectivity'.

Measured Connectors believe that people in successful and responsive organizations are constantly communicating with each other, rather than waiting for directives from above. These leaders pay attention to connectivity by bringing people together, and helping the organization to understand its sense of purpose and important ground-rules.

Research findings

- Very widely used by effective leaders.
- Eighteen per cent of the leaders in our survey named this role as the most attractive leadership role model.
- A popular choice as a boss.
- Nearly half of the leaders in our survey said this was their natural leadership role.
- Only six per cent of the leaders in our survey named this role as the hardest to adopt.
- Measured Connectors find the Edgy Catalyser and Visionary Motivator roles the most difficult to access.
- Useful role in many situations, but particularly when there are multiple partners and stakeholders involved, when cultural change is required or when morale is low. Not so useful in organizational turnarounds.

ALL ABOUT THE MEASURED CONNECTOR ROLE

When performing the Measured Connector role, the leader focuses on connecting a myriad of different agendas and helping to create a common sense of meaning. This leader is able to deal with multiple stakeholders and competing objectives in a calm and focused way, slowly creating trust, taking an interest in people's needs and motivations, testing alignment and continuing to move things forward towards action. They can act as a focal point, around which people can gather. Their patterns of influence are steady and always about moving people towards the areas of common interest and encouraging small experiments and early prototypes to emerge.

Often seen as in the eye of the storm, rather than the storm itself, the Measured Connector influences people in an unruffled and unhurried way. Through maintaining people's focus on the important few strategic issues, the Measured Connector helps people to reflect on their roles and activities, to broaden their perspectives through meeting with others they would not otherwise connect with, and to take action to try new things out.

The Measured Connector is often very well respected within the organization, displaying authenticity and an ability to remove obstacles quietly through subtle influencing of key players. This type of leader doesn't play power politics by hiding information or building support in order to undermine others, but instead creates feedback loops and encourages people to find out things for themselves. The instinct is to want others to know more about the reality of a situation. Neither does he or she tie activities up in red tape, preferring people to be free to try things out on a small scale before any major planning process kicks in.

A typical example of a Measured Connector is the public sector leader who at any one time will most likely have multiple goals and outcomes on a range of policy initiatives. The good leaders can successfully collaborate with a number of significant external partners across a range of different public and private organizations to achieve joint aims. Many leaders are impatient for hard outcomes, or have a tendency to over-control situations. This makes it almost impossible for them to be successful in a multi-stakeholder environment. The Measured Connector is instead patient and interested, tapping into people's interests and drive, and empowering them to become part of something bigger.

Peter Senge *et al*'s book *Presence* identifies the importance of experimenting and prototyping to enable change to progress, and suggests that staying connected becomes a strategic priority to achieve coherence amongst potentially fragmented streams of activity. The calmness that a Measured Connector maintains is also seen as important by Senge. He calls it 'mindfulness' and describes this state of being as a kind of stillness that enables a leader to focus without reactivity or agitation, and in a non-judgemental way.

Malcolm Gladwell's fascinating book *The Tipping Point* looks at how small, seemingly insignificant actions can lead to significant change. He identifies the three types of people who are vital links in the process of creating significant change, and names one the 'Connector'. He says that Connectors are people who build relationships with ease and have a natural ability to keep in touch with these people over time. They know so many people from so many different worlds that they have the effect of bringing them together. It's their ability to communicate a message very quickly to many people that makes them so significant in the change process.

Gladwell says that step change is often catalysed by just a small number of Connectors. He explains the Connector's approach by saying: 'These people see possibility while most of us are busily choosing whom we would like to know, and rejecting the people who don't look right or who live out near the airport, or whom we haven't seen in sixty-five years... Connectors like them all.' This is a very similar mentality to the Measured Connector.

HEART AND SOUL OF THE MEASURED CONNECTOR ROLE

The Measured Connector is an affirming and appreciative presence in organizational life. These leaders deeply value the creation of a shared understanding of purpose through collective sensemaking, believing that interconnectedness is extremely important. They think and feel systemically, thus combining a reflectiveness with an awareness of when action is necessary. They seek to bring disparate people together for a clear purpose, and value the synergy that results from this. Collaboration is therefore a key concern.

The calmness allows their inherent authenticity and genuineness to show. They are more likely to adopt a 'low-key' but well-framed approach than to deliberately create waves or see the need to manage people particularly closely. They value self-awareness and social awareness and believe that a high level of emotional intelligence is essential if leaders are to lead well.

THE MEASURED CONNECTOR'S INNER EXPERIENCE

What they're thinking

Measured Connectors are able to embrace a situation fully and are able to understand but not be overly concerned about the number of stakeholders or the multiplicity of agendas. They are interested in learning about other people's concerns and able to weigh these up in a dispassionate way, rooting out the interests and pockets of energy that will help to further the common strategic aims. They never tire of bringing people together, and encouraging information flow and exchange of ideas. Their interest is not in controlling these interactions but in emphasizing the common purpose that binds the entire community together and encouraging people to take small actions where they feel ready to do so.

How they're feeling

Measured Connectors are good at staying calm when it matters. Natural Measured Connectors are able to do this effortlessly, whereas others have learnt to achieve this kind of stillness by deliberately finding a quiet moment when they can switch off from outside interference. They may feel a constant impetus about needing to make progress and get things done, but experience tells them that the best way to implement change is to encourage people to exchange and work things out for themselves, and to give them a strong strategic steer as a guide.

THE MEASURED CONNECTOR'S OUTER PRESENTATION

Posture

The posture of the Measured Connector is alert but relaxed. They are unlikely to sit on the edge of their seat or tap their feet. Neither do they sit right back in their seats in a languid switched-out pose. They are calmly interested, maintaining good eye contact with everyone in the room, and taking up enough space without claiming too much territory by sprawling on their seats or putting their belongings all over the place. They are very respectful of other people's space.

Upsides

Measured Connectors can deal well with ambiguity, paradox and slow decision-making processes. They can manage their own emotions well when they need to and can be temporarily dispassionate about their own passions in order to focus on someone else's agenda. The Measured Connector can adapt well to different audiences, drawing out themes and telling stories that bring threads of ideas together. These leaders are exceptionally good one-to-one communicators.

Downsides

Measured Connectors are so focused on the big picture, and on connecting and dealing with complexity, that they may not get around to the necessary short-term actions. Rigorous monitoring of activity is not their forte. They prefer authentic relationships and find that political game-playing is difficult for them.

Measured Connectors generally have to rely on others to look after the financial and performance-related details. They can also become scattered or thinly spread and have to work hard at being visible to all the key stakeholders.

What they're not

Measured Connectors can sometimes be erroneously described as 'laid back' or 'lacking in ambition'. If leaders truly are Measured Connectors, they are neither laid back nor lacking in ambition. This is not a passive role. Neither can it be carried out by someone who lacks the ambition and the commitment to achieve the organization's goals. However, it does require an ability to subjugate one's own ego for a while, and allow others to shine – even to allow others to take the helm if appropriate.

Measured Connectors have extraordinary energy for pursuing organizational goals, but this is coupled with patience, and a realization that the Lone Ranger attitude of 'I can do it all myself' is fallacious. The Measured Connector recognizes that the development of honest, adult partnerships is the key to real progress.

ORGANIZATIONAL ASPECTS OF THE MEASURED CONNECTOR ROLE

Every organizational environment or 'culture' is subtly different and the Measured Connector must adapt a little to the culture if he or she is to be successful.

How can the Measured Connector adapt his or her style? He or she needs to be able to conform just enough to keep to the organizational ground-rules without losing the ability to share power and develop a new sense of purpose across different parties and to bring momentum and energy to a complex and possibly overwhelming situation. It will be necessary to avoid the very real possibility of being slowed down to a crawling pace by organizational politics or red tape, or the danger of under-delivering in a very task-focused output-driven environment.

In a mechanistic organization, facts and outputs matter more than relationships, and the Measured Connector will need to deliver visible outputs and develop credibility before starting to work on strengthening relationships across functional or departmental boundaries. The Measured Connector needs to realize that conversations between individuals will not be enough to catalyse action in a mechanistic organization, no matter how significant they seem at the time. There will also need to be a business case with sound rationale that all parties understand and sign off.

The Measured Connector will only be successful in a political culture if sponsored by powerful people. That means talking to these people first to ensure their buy-in before involving others. This may seem manipulative, but is key to success. These conversations will typically be honest and up front. Support will be asked for on the basis of a sound rationale.

It's especially important for the Measured Connector to be authentic and consistent in a political organization, where it is sometimes hard to know whom to trust. Leaders who are 'new kids on the block' in political organizations are not really taken seriously as Measured Connectors unless they are seen to be authentic and truly working for the advancement of organizational goals. The suspicion will be that the leader is simply building support for their own agenda, or advancement of their own career.

Measured Connectors are often most at home in a messy or fluid culture. This type of culture allows cross-organizational discussion and encourages experimentation. The only area that may need to be boosted for the Measured Connector to be successful in this type of environment is the way in which they communicate their sense of purpose – preferably in an attractive, coherent and energetic way. Fluid organizations are so fast and well connected that change only happens when an issue resonates with people's current experiences and catches their attention fairly quickly. Thus the Measured Connector needs to be energetic and clear. If no one is interested in their agenda the best thing to do is to back off and rethink the approach.

In adaptive cultures, the Measured Connector may find that there is already an established way of connecting people and things, and may have to work hard to break through these processes that are already in place for creating organizational change. He or she will need to encourage well-supported experimentation on a small scale to get people to experience things differently. For example, an organization that uses customer surveys every year to inform their sales agenda may have become rather stuck and over-comfortable in this potentially unproductive cycle. The Measured Connector may want to encourage different conversations to take place, and small experiments to happen with a view to uncovering issues and developing a common understanding of what needs to be addressed.

EXAMPLES OF MEASURED CONNECTORS

Virgin boss Sir Richard Branson regularly uses the Measured Connector role. He is said to be a herder of cats rather than a leader of sheep. He gets to know people, gets to trust them and then creates a challenging environment for them. What he doesn't do is breathe down their necks or tell them what to do. He helps them to get set up, connecting them with others and providing key resources.

Richard Branson's Measured Connector role is also demonstrated by his great belief in working with family and friends. Even his ex-wife is apparently included in the roll-call of colleagues. Many of us would see huge risks in this; he sees only advantages. This makes him a true Measured Connector, who thrives on bringing trusted, energetic people together and connecting different worlds to create something new and vibrant. The structure he has created at Virgin is unusual. It consists of more than 500 small companies around the world operating independently. This is similar to the Japanese *keiretsu* system in which many small companies interlock within a collaborative network.

Tim Smit is chief executive and co-founder of the Eden Project in Cornwall. When he first began to try to get this extraordinary project off the ground he had to pay a great deal of attention to being a Measured Connector. The project was to transform a disused china-clay pit into a living theatre of plants and people, and a refuge for the world's endangered plant species. He had to convince funders, inspire sponsors, entice the right technical experts and ensure that the local people supported the enterprise.

He says about trying to connect with the locals: 'Cornish people are so egalitarian, they will have no truck with incomers saying you need to make changes. It's about respect. If you do something new and show people respect before doing it, you could not wish for friendlier people. That helped us at the Eden Project. We listened to the public, which made it better.'

Smit discovered exactly how crucial the need to connect different agendas was by talking to people who had attempted a similar project in Wales. The Ebbw Vale Garden Festival organizers had experienced disappointing visitor numbers. The main problem appeared to be the lack of integration between the different stakeholders, such as the County Council, District Council, Welsh Development Agency and

English Partnership. In the end, the garden had opened on time, but the railway line stopped a mile and a half short of the site and there were no hotels nearby. It was as if the project had been completed to the letter, but none of the linking pieces were in place.

Barbara Stocking is Director of Oxfam, a development, relief and campaigning organization that works with others to overcome poverty and suffering around the world. Oxfam runs projects in over 70 countries, working alongside over 100 different agencies and partners. The organization supports the Make Poverty History campaign along with 450 other organizations, which is part of a global call to action against poverty. Barbara is a great example of someone whose job requires her to operate as a Measured Connector.

She says of the organization's work, 'We are proud to be part of a huge, diverse coalition. Together we are making a significant impact... Europe's promise to double aid by 2010 is at least partly the coalition's doing.' She puts energy into helping different agendas to come together, using a complex combination of lobbying and public petitions and campaigns and work on the ground. One day she may be engaged in detailed discussion with the director of the International Monetary Fund; 24 hours later she may be in the middle of a field in a West African country, talking to local people. In this way she, and her colleagues, can help to bring different views and agendas together and help create progress.

Several years ago we worked with the global IT director of a large oil company who used the Measured Connector role a great deal. Her challenge was to get the 2,000-strong company-wide IT community to respond to board-level pressure to outsource many services and eventually to reduce IT staff numbers. This was a tricky issue. However, she approached it with respect and empathy. She wanted to be up front about what lay ahead, and to assure people that outsourcing could mean new opportunities for them. She also acknowledged that there would be sadness and maybe anger for those who might have to leave the company that had trained them up and looked after them so well.

She commissioned a three-day event that brought the top 100 IT managers together to discuss the issues they were all facing and to start to come up with solutions. She resisted the temptation to lead this event too strongly, instead preferring to take a back seat and move around the conference, visiting different groups during the many workshops, asking questions and attempting to understand people's perspectives.

During one workshop, a cross-cutting group of IT folks were having a heated discussion about the different options available for providing a particular service. One of the participants said out of sheer frustration, 'Let's find out what the director thinks. Where is she?' He started looking around the room. At that point I saw the director hide behind one of the huge marble pillars. She put her finger to her lips, looked at me, and whispered 'Shush! I want them to work this out for themselves.' This is one way to really get people to work out a common agenda!

Another Measured Connector we know well is the finance director within a large UK Civil Service department. His job involves making significant changes to internal systems and to fundamental work practices to significantly increase the professionalism of the finance function throughout the organization. Many senior people within the organization find these changes problematic. They involve greater visibility and accountability for them, and a painful and disruptive process of change which makes day-to-day delivery difficult.

This leader is highly energetic and driven, but he exudes calmness and patience when others are losing their cool. He makes it his business to get to know people, and to find out what they are trying to achieve. However, his masterful skill is his ability to put people together to discuss the right issues. This process may seem muddled and chaotic to those involved. It may even be frustrating, especially when the people being 'connected' don't always fully understand his intentions. Significantly, as with other Measured Connectors, this leader's intentions are a little fluid, and although there is a core of key principles, the order and manner in which he goes about things is highly flexible.

This finance director's success lies in his ability to endure chaos over time and contain it within clear boundaries. He knows that this will lead to good results eventually and the chaos doesn't distract him at all. He spends time edging people along, and tailoring agendas to suit the key players. What he doesn't do is worry unduly about whether or not an output was achieved today in a certain way.

Sven-Goran Eriksson was England's national football team coach for five years. His leadership style is described as professional, understated and calm. He affected an icy cool on the touchline when managing the England football team, which was interpreted as lack of passion by some commentators.

He is said to motivate players through trust, focus and a positive attitude. The book *Leadership the Sven-Goran Eriksson Way* (Birkinshaw and Crainer, 2002), describes his style as providing clear boundaries with enough structure to hold the team together and sufficient freedom for the players to experiment and grow. It is rumoured that there was a lot of sniping and unrest between team members when Eriksson was in charge, which he never spoke about to the press. He tried to tackle things quietly and in an adult fashion, typical of the Measured Connector.

Eriksson was viciously attacked by the press during his five years as England manager, even though his performance was reasonably good. Expectations, as always in football, were ridiculously high. But now when he is interviewed by the UK press he is calm and gracious, as if nothing ever happened between them.

Sir Menzies Campbell led the Liberal Democrats in the UK for only 18 months but was said to have brought stability and a sense of purpose to the party. He professionalized the internal operations of the party and helped prepare the party for a general election. He was never a fiery, motivating speaker, but instead exuded calmness and was praised for his integrity.

Bill Clinton was known as the master connector; good at meeting people, remembering facts that connected ideas and people, and able to understand an issue very thoroughly. His Visionary Motivator role appears to be quite strong, but there's a Measured Connector role there in the shadows too.

8

The Tenacious Implementer

THE TENACIOUS IMPLEMENTER ROLE IN A NUTSHELL

'Just follow the plan and we'll get this done.'

- Doggedly pursues the plan.
- Holds people to account.
- Leads by driving a project through to completion.
- Focuses on 'the project'.

Delivery to time, quality and budget is the main focus of the Tenacious Implementer. They believe that when day-to-day delivery is on track, organizations tend to experience success.

Research findings

- Best used in small doses.
- Positively correlated with the Edgy Catalyser role.
- Only six per cent of the leaders in our survey named this role as their natural leadership role.
- Often seen in organizational life (but not necessarily done that well?).
- Thirty per cent of respondents named this role as the hardest to adopt.
- The hardest role for a Visionary Motivator to perform tends to be the Tenacious Implementer role, and vice versa.
- Not seen as an attractive role model, or as a popular boss to have.
- Tenacious Implementers tend to admire Visionary Motivators and Thoughtful Architects.
- Useful role in many situations, but particularly when the change is well defined eg technology-led change, a critical project, tighter compliance, new legislation, specific process improvement initiatives.

ALL ABOUT THE TENACIOUS IMPLEMENTER ROLE

The Tenacious Implementer makes sure things get done. In this role, the leader is seen as the driving force for the implementation of the agreed plan. This is often described as the classic Project Manager or Programme Manager role. These leaders are renowned for their ability to mobilize other people in service of a plan. They know the milestones, understand the key aims and are au fait with enough of the technical information behind the project that they can be useful integrators at a top level when needed.

Tenacious Implementers are logical, good with facts and detail, able to think strategically and look ahead, but very much focused on making something significant happen and making it sustainable. They are not happy until all the necessary elements are in place, including documentation and final reviews. Restless and full of a pragmatic brand of energy, they thrive on long hours and lots of technical challenges, and they particularly enjoy being invited to sort out a big technical or managerial mess.

When it comes to people issues, their first tactic is to wear down the resisters using persuasive logic. They can marshal the facts quickly to defeat an opponent in an argument, and their sheer will to win often impresses. They tend to manage stakeholders as a careful car owner might manage all the moving parts in the car engine. This process involves maintaining relationships regularly, using regular conversations which can appear a bit forced and dogged. Tenacious Implementers may 'bang on' about the same issues again and again until the other person gives in.

Tenacious Implementers are always in touch with task-related progress. They tend to insist on regular, structured reporting, and good up-front discussions about the problems which result in agreed action. They also ensure that sophisticated feedback loops are in place so that everyone knows on a monthly basis what is to be done and why. Communications to the stakeholder group are clear and well planned.

Much of the popular leadership literature suggests that Tenacious Implementers are somehow less valuable than other types of leader. The implication is that 'real leadership' involves more long-range thinking, visionary capacity, radical innovation and strategic partnership building, and that the Tenacious Implementer's work is 'operational' and therefore less worthwhile. However, our research (see Part 3) indicates that this role is the most effective of the five roles when leading change initiatives such as business process reengineering; leading the design and launch of a new product; and leading critical technology-based projects. In fact, the Tenacious Implementer role was seen as the most significant leadership role in ensuring success in over 25 per cent of the change initiatives that were currently under way for our questionnaire respondents.

Prosci's influential research into best practice in change management in 2003 (www.prosci.com) listed the top five organizational contributors to change management success. Two of these are clearly areas that Tenacious Implementers bring to the leadership role with ease. These are: *a well-planned and organized approach*, and *continuous and targeted communication.* Far from being simple cogs in the wheel of change, subservient to the visionaries at the top, the Tenacious Implementers provide a focused, purposeful leadership which works well when the change required is either highly technical, or fairly well defined.

We believe that the work of Tenacious Implementers is undervalued, and that high-level strategic work is often overvalued. We often see the so-called visionary or strategic leader just drifting above the surface of important change work, not getting to grips with anything or adding any real value, frightened to admit to not really knowing what's going on.

HEART AND SOUL OF THE TENACIOUS IMPLEMENTER

The Tenacious Implementer values loyalty to an agreed purpose or plan. The Tenacious Implementer has very high integrity and is completely trustworthy. These people are solid and reliable, often providing a high level of work ethic from which others around them benefit. High priorities are being methodical, being structured and being systematic. They don't necessarily value speed but instead appreciate tenacity, perseverance and achievement of outcomes.

These leaders don't court change for change's sake, because they have an ultimate practical goal in mind. They are therefore very 'hands on' and constantly seek ways to make things better. They are not necessarily bureaucratic, but if there is a procedure or an existing rule, they will be keen to use it pragmatically rather than circumvent it for the sake of speed.

They value honesty and courage and are not afraid to apply a bit of pressure if they see that people are resistant to making an effort. However, they do value people's contributions and are loyal to people who are reliable co-workers and to people who are genuinely trying to do their best for the project or the organization.

THE TENACIOUS IMPLEMENTER'S INNER EXPERIENCE

What they're thinking

Tenacious Implementers are always thinking about what needs to be done next. They have very full diaries, and a tendency to try to fit more things in and keep to quite aggressive timescales. Their meetings and phone calls will be short and to the point. Don't expect a lot of social chit-chat. They tend to think linearly and sequentially, although that's not to say that they don't factor people and possibilities into their plans.

How they're feeling

They get irritated with lack of delivery and become especially wound up by false promises or unpleasant surprises. Skilled Tenacious Implementers do not show their irritation. They simply ask pertinent, direct questions and breathe down people's necks until things get done.

THE TENACIOUS IMPLEMENTER'S OUTER PRESENTATION

Posture

Tenacious Implementers will spend their time either sitting, working on a plan in a totally focused way, or in a meeting, slightly forward in their seats, maintaining a lot of eye contact, ensuring that the agenda is followed exactly. They tend to sit squarely, maybe with their hands on their knees, maybe with clenched fists, ready to go to the next appointment once agreement has been reached.

Upsides

Tenacious Implementers are very focused, well planned and beautifully organized. They are able to select just the right performance indicators and manage these well, having the ability to truly stick with the plan; like a dog with a bone. They are great colleagues to have because they are so reliable and clear.

Downsides

Tenacious Implementers can be a bit too forceful. They are so keen to hear people say 'yes' that they can start to find 'no' impossible to hear. They might resort to talking _at_ people to try to turn them around, instead of exploring options or helping to clarify what's in the way.

When an unforeseen obstacle arises, the Tenacious Implementer always prefers a workaround to a complete redesign. This can be the Tenacious Implementer's Achilles' heel because on occasions, a workaround just isn't possible. However, in discussion, the Tenacious Implementer can dominate the conversation and shut off the possibility of looking at new options. Given their level of focus on task outcome, they may be tempted to drive things forward and through any obstacles, which can of course be people as well as situations.

What they're not

Tenacious Implementers are not purely automatons or dictators. This leadership role ceases to be a _leadership_ role when the humanity is taken out and an individual operates in a totally task-focused way, like a machine, demanding that things are done their way and ignoring other views and wishes.

Neither are Tenacious Implementers obsessive perfectionists, seeking refuge in the minute details of a project. That would be an impossible approach to leading anything; the leader would never be able to see the wood for the trees. What Tenacious Implementers are able to do is understand the mass of detail enough, and then chunk it up into manageable units of progress.

ORGANIZATIONAL ASPECTS OF THE TENACIOUS IMPLEMENTER ROLE

Every organizational environment or 'culture' is uniquely different and the Tenacious Implementer must adapt a little to the culture if he or she is to be successful.

How can the Tenacious Implementer adapt his or her style? It's important for the Tenacious Implementer to be able to be versatile interpersonally to cope with different environments. Flexibility of approach is also important to enable effective working in more fluid types of organization. The common pitfall for the inflexible Tenacious Implementer is to be seen as too blinkered and dogged, and thus fail to get the support that's needed from colleagues.

The Tenacious Implementer may feel most at home in a mechanistic environment. Very often, significant change in a mechanistic setting involves more cross-functional conversation and connection than normal. The Tenacious Implementer will need to find a way of breaking down silos by creating well-planned opportunities for people to talk productively across the boundaries.

In a political culture, the Tenacious Implementer needs to remember how important stakeholders really are. Success will not come through delivering results alone, as that is not how the world is in political environments. The right stakeholders need to be on board, and visible sponsorship needs to be in place. Coalitions and alliances may need to be built and sustained and key stakeholders' needs and wants factored into the final plans.

In a messy or fluid culture, the Tenacious Implementer may need to suspend his or her need for certainty and predictability, and learn to delegate and trust more than may be comfortable. Skills in definition and control, and the ability to set clear boundaries and frameworks to guide others, will be useful. For example, this might mean putting project milestones and a purpose in place, together with a set of key principles to be followed, and then asking people to come up with their own plans and timescales. This replaces intensive planning meetings at which many details are pored over.

In an adaptive culture, the Tenacious Implementer may get into trouble for being too forceful with managers and front-line workers, or for being too hard on the customer. In an adaptive organization, the focus is on healthy development and well-designed approaches in response to feedback. The Tenacious Implementer needs to learn to respect this approach, tapping into the clear objectives that appeal to adaptive organizations, by organizing clear communication and feedback loops, and setting up 'hot-house' projects to move the pace along more quickly.

EXAMPLES OF TENACIOUS IMPLEMENTERS

Vladimir Putin, former President of the Russian Federation, is a Tenacious Implementer. He achieved a great deal after taking office on 31 December 1999 and has a reputation for being a man who gets things done. His high popularity rating in Russia speaks for itself. His rating remained high throughout his presidency, never falling below 65 per cent, even though he has been heavily criticized by the West for having an anti-democratic approach.

The Russian people regard Vladimir Putin's foreign policy achievements as his main success, according to the results of a recent poll carried out by the *Public Opinion* foundation. In addition, on the home front, particular mention was given to his move to increase the pay of public sector workers and to increase state pensions. 'On the whole, people have begun to live better' said those questioned.

In press conferences, Putin is impressive, fielding questions in an energetic and commanding fashion. One of his renowned marathon press conferences, held in front of 1,232 Russian and foreign journalists, lasted three and a half hours. Putin was very much in control, reeling off economic indicators with great ease and accuracy. This command of the facts is a sure sign of a Tenacious Implementer.

Another Tenacious Implementer, Evelyn Thurlby, was vital to the success of the Eden Project, a vast and complex project to transform a disused china-clay pit into a living theatre of plants and people. The delivery vehicle for Cornwall's great success story was Eden Project Ltd. Thurlby was appointed CEO for her ability to bring the Tenacious Implementer role to this enormously complex project. She established rigorous reporting processes, painful for some people, but necessary to give the board and existing and prospective funders confidence about project progress.

In his account of the extraordinary project, Tim Smit describes Evelyn with admiration and just a touch of irritation. He says:

> Evelyn was just what the project needed: tough, driven and focused. While her full-blooded approach made me swallow hard on occasion, and her impatience to dispense with pleasantries sometimes felt like fingernails running down a blackboard, she was right that the project needed to become professional. What drove her mad were the myriad connections that were nurtured for no immediate gain, with a view to a bigger future at some indefinable point. Where I saw a campaign, she saw it broken down into individual battles that had to be won along the way. The truth is we were both right, and without both tactics being employed in tandem we would never have made the progress we did.

(See Chapter 7 for a description of Tim Smit's leadership style.)

We worked with a very successful CEO who grew a software engineering company from very small beginnings to a successful international organization, using the Tenacious Implementer as his main leadership role. It took him 10 years to grow the company, but he made it. With his trademark neatly clipped beard and perfectly trimmed hair, and his incredibly stubborn approach, he nudged projects along and kept the right stakeholders interested and on board. He had his plan for the company, and doggedly pursued it, no matter what diversions came his way. His command of technical detail was impressive, and he was able to describe the work on all the significant company projects, and name the individuals that worked on them.

Early on in his role as CEO he discovered a couple of weak areas in his style which were driving his colleagues to distraction. The first was his habit of going to a meeting with his mind made up and his ears switched off, unable to hear anyone else's idea. The second was his need for everything that left the building to be 100 per cent perfect, including letters, proposals, and the like. You name it; he had to make it perfect. His staff and colleagues thought that the latter was often a waste of effort, especially for discussion documents or draft proposals.

He confided in me that this feedback had troubled him, and following some days of contemplation and worry he came up with two simple solutions. The first was to enter every meeting with two plans, both of which he liked equally well. This tactic gave the impression of someone who was willing to consider at least two options. He was then able to discuss these two options and be equally happy whichever way the meeting decided. His other masterstroke was to tame his own perfectionism using the '70 per cent technique'. This meant that he made a rule for himself and others that non-critical outputs could leave the building if they were 70 per cent correct. That would be good enough. This is how a Tenacious Implementer socializes himself!

Another Tenacious Implementer that we know well is a highly respected and extremely successful regional director for a large international steel company. He is so successful at rescuing steel businesses that his recent attempts to retire have been met with a string of requests to carry on as a consultant and mentor to other aspiring regional directors. He is driven, energetic, masterful with the facts and capable, when necessary, of being as stubborn as the day is long.

His first action on entering a business is to establish performance targets and get a rigorous, regular process for monitoring how the business is doing. He says that if that can't be done you might as well go home. This is a painful process for a management team that isn't used to rigour. This is the way a Tenacious Implementer operates; he breaks things down into understandable chunks and visible measurements. Win the battle by tackling one skirmish at a time.

This Tenacious Implementer leader is extremely good at stakeholder management. He does this via a carefully planned series of regular short meetings with key people; using the same techniques for people who are internal and external to the organization. He always has a list of agenda items and he will be sure to cover them. If he needs something done he will chip away at the individual with an 'I'm sure you agree we need to draw up a plan for…' or 'I think the best thing you can do is to have a quiet chat with…' He is very hard to resist!

The greatest strength of this leader, beyond his well-honed technical and managerial skills, is his self-awareness. He recognizes his own heavy task-focus and has developed his interpersonal skills to a high level; he has trained himself to be respectful and patient with others. He has learned to temper his own need for pace and directness. He is a great model of a successful Tenacious Implementer who has adapted himself in order to become extremely successful.

Warren Buffett is a key exemplar of this role. One of the richest business investors in the world, he is very pragmatic, focused and tough-minded, and certainly someone who doesn't subscribe to the cult of celebrity. He obsesses about getting things right and is willing to persevere until that happens. He gets very involved and closely monitors all of his transactions and contributes his business savvy wherever he can. He maintains that he doesn't ever invest in a business that he doesn't understand.

Martin Sorrell is CEO of WPP, one of the world's largest communications services groups, which employs more than 100,000 people worldwide. He's an exceptionally driven man and very focused, who uses the Tenacious Implementer role with great skill. However, he says the key quality of a successful CEO is persistence. He told a CNN reporter:

> Yes, they've described me as being a micro-manager which I think is a compliment not an insult. I don't think I drive people crazy, I just think detail's important. I think accuracy's important... I came across a quote by Calvin Coolidge... about persistence. Basically it said... there are a lot of people who are unsuccessful who are intelligent, there are a lot of people who are successful who aren't well educated, but in his view the common quality was persistence... I think doing things, executing quickly is important, not delaying. I always think delayers are negative.

A different way of approaching the Tenacious Implementer role is illustrated by Michael Dell, founder and CEO of Dell, Inc. The company became the most profitable PC manufacturer in the world in 2004, with sales of $49 billion and profits of $3 billion. But the work is never done for Michael Dell. He talks now about forging a company that will last well into the future, after he's gone. This is one of the signs of the Tenacious Implementer; there is always work still to be done.

Michael Dell has studied business history in some detail, and is careful about his investments. He says he is not interested in the next exciting innovation; he is more interested in building the current product, as well and as cheaply as possible. One of the dangerous pitfalls of the Tenacious Implementer role is the propensity to get caught up in single-track thinking. However, Dell is able to be strategically agile as well as being dogged and focused. He is able to change tack very swiftly if he thinks it's necessary. For instance, in 2001, he abandoned a plan to enter the mobile-phone market six months after hiring a top executive from Motorola to head it up, deciding that the prospects weren't well starred enough to justify the costs of entry.

He's courageous too. If something needs facing, he will face it and make a plan to address things. On receiving critical feedback about his distant and cold style, Dell faced his top 20 managers and offered a frank self-critique, acknowledging that he is hugely shy and that it sometimes made him seem aloof and unapproachable. He promised to communicate with the team much more closely. Dell is also refreshingly realistic about his non-charismatic personality. Once, after hearing about the exploits of the flamboyant Oracle CEO, Lawrence J Ellison, he held up a piece of paper and said, 'See this? It's vanilla and square, and so am I.'

George Washington could also display Tenacious Implementer qualities, described by one of his colleagues in glowing terms: 'If you speak of solid information and sound judgment, Colonel Washington is undoubtedly the greatest man present.' He held his small group of volunteers together through many years of deprivation and bitter onslaught from the British army. His key qualities were his ability to keep his men together under difficult conditions by maintaining their focus on an end-goal; his ability to maximize the use of scarce resources; and his excellent logistical and project management skills.

Gordon Brown, prime minister of the UK, is a Tenacious Implementer at times too. He is dogged and dour, irritated by flippancy and prone to getting annoyed when an agreed plan is taken off course. His speeches lack the sparkle of a Visionary Motivator, but some voters warm to his no-nonsense, 'spin-free' way of communicating. Brown's first couple of months as prime minister were plagued by crisis after crisis; floods, foot and mouth disease, terrorist attacks. He was seen to handle all this extremely well. He is a natural planner and responds to a crisis. He expertly gets the resources together and agrees the plan.

Brown's achievements throughout his career have been due to his ability to stick with the plan. He presided as Chancellor of the Exchequer over the longest-ever period of growth in the UK. Said to have iron determination, his experience of having a detached retina at the age of 16 appeared to have a big impact on him. His older brother John said in a recent interview, 'It made him more determined. He was in more of a hurry; he feared he might lose his sight altogether. It was a bleak experience.'

9

The Thoughtful Architect

THE THOUGHTFUL ARCHITECT ROLE IN A NUTSHELL

'Let me explain the key concepts and frameworks.'

- Is principal architect and designer of strategies.

- Crafts seemingly disparate ideas into a way forward.

- Scans the environment, sees what's happening in the environment and creates an organizing framework.

- Focuses on 'the design'.

Supply chains, customer loyalty programmes, global IT solutions, shared service centres, community development programmes… these things all need to be conceived and designed. Thoughtful Architects focus on creating the concepts that lie behind strategic plans and designing new processes and operating models.

Research findings

- Best used in small doses.
- Eighteen per cent of the leaders in our survey named this role as their natural leadership role.
- Twelve per cent of respondents named this role as the hardest to adopt.
- Thoughtful Architects tend to find the Edgy Catalyser role the hardest one to access.
- Twenty-six per cent of respondents named this as the most attractive role model.
- Thoughtful Architects tend to find the Visionary Motivator to be the most attractive role model.
- One of the least frequently observed styles in organizational life.
- Useful role particularly in complex organizational change, or when working on a long-range strategy. Least useful when morale is low, or there is a critical project to deliver.

ALL ABOUT THE THOUGHTFUL ARCHITECT ROLE

The Thoughtful Architect leads through creating a clear strategy based on original thinking. These leaders can craft seemingly disconnected ideas into a viable way forward, and can invent and think through radical new ways of working. They are often seen as the principal strategist and designer of grand plans, holding the bigger picture in their heads throughout the process.

In order to achieve this, the Thoughtful Architect displays certain qualities and characteristics. They are able to take a 'helicopter view' of the situation. This involves scanning both the internal and external environments, picking up on patterns and making connections. With this helicopter view they can see current and future scenarios from both an internal and an external perspective. They then analyse the data, appraise the situation and synthesize new frameworks.

They are focused and use the information they glean in the here and now to build visions and strategies for the future. They work at a high level and may be short on some of the detail. They will look inside themselves, or to an established expert, for a theory or model in which to encapsulate what it is they are striving for. They can be conventional, radical, mechanistic or innovative in their thinking, but they will strive to build a vision or a strategy in a way that is coherent and fits together well.

They are likely to appear rather introverted, though that's not to say they don't have passion for their vision. They are initially internally focused, building the concepts in their heads or on paper before they are ready to announce them to the world. They value depth and rigour of thought and won't abide sloppy or inconsistent thinking or illogical plans. As they are interested in developing expertise and competence they also see learning as a continual process, and will typically be open to new ideas.

THE HEART AND SOUL OF THE
THOUGHTFUL ARCHITECT

Thoughtful Architects value concepts and ideas, models and frameworks. They respect expertise and competence and arguments which 'stack up' and have an inner consistency. They are looking to achieve mastery in what they do and to be seen as credible and competent designers of a new world, sometimes thinking of themselves as being involved in noble work, rather than what they see as the inconsequential day-to-day mess of activity.

They value others who have honed an area of expertise, or who have obviously taken care to think through the implications of their plans and actions and who can demonstrate a consistency and coherence in their approach. They value people who are specialist and have a high level of competence in their field.

THE THOUGHTFUL ARCHITECT'S INNER EXPERIENCE

What they're thinking

The Thoughtful Architect thinks much of the time! That is his or her primary mode of being. And in so doing these leaders attempt to make sense of the world that they see, and try to find a model, a plan or a framework in which to order it. They are natural reflectors, spending time reviewing the current situation and scanning the horizon. They are also natural theorists, making connections and seeing the bigger picture by putting the current situation into the wider context. They will have grand thoughts and be constantly trying to build models of the future into which they can confidently direct people.

How they're feeling

Thoughtful Architects can be hard to read sometimes, as their emotions are often well contained, indeed concealed. They themselves may be somewhat out of touch with their own feelings when it comes to interacting with others, which may make them seem cold or distant. However, their overriding passion will be to create strategies that work and a future that makes sense. Get them talking about the future and you will see their passion revealed.

Because they want to make sense of things first, they come up with plans which are already well thought out. This can lead to potential conflict with others as they may not truly offer the chance to influence the outcome. Given that the Thoughtful Architect is more likely to favour the inner world rather than the outer world, interactions and engagement with others may take a back seat.

THE THOUGHTFUL ARCHITECT'S OUTER PRESENTATION

Posture

Thoughtful Architects can appear slow moving and pensive. They will be quite quiet with a degree of detachment – sometimes just observing the world, at other times seemingly lost in their own thoughts. Eye contact might be difficult, either because they are in-turned or distracted by something in the environment. They may be hesitant to commit to a view as they take their time to process data and comments, but they can be very determined once they've thought something through.

Upsides

Thoughtful Architects are great assets when you really want to think through your options. Their ability to step into the future and create a vision and complementary strategy which factors in today's data and tomorrow's possible scenarios is second to none. Because of their thoroughness you know that their analyses and their designs will be well thought out.

Downsides

There can be a tendency for the Thoughtful Architect to take their time over things – always looking into the future, thinking it through, ensuring there is an inner consistency and developing a strategy. There isn't much time or energy for reactive leadership, or deciding on tactics for today. The Thoughtful Architect can thus be not very spontaneous and might let opportunities slip by. They need time and space, and these are often in short supply. They can also favour the purity of the strategy over the impact on people, and sometimes the needs, wishes and feelings of others are not factored in.

Sometimes they seem to be so clever that others suspect their motives, whether this is justified or not. They can be seen as 'too clever by half'. The problem is that they don't always spend enough time investing in relationships and partnerships which are explicitly and jointly committed to a common endeavour, which would help to counteract the suspicions.

What they're not

Thoughtful Architects are not necessarily geniuses, or entirely original thinkers. Neither are they socially incompetent, or living in an ivory tower. If that were the case they wouldn't be able to lead.

ORGANIZATIONAL ASPECTS OF THOUGHTFUL ARCHITECTS

Every organizational environment or 'culture' is subtly different and the Thoughtful Architect must adapt a little to the culture if he or she is to be successful.

How can the Thoughtful Architect adapt his or her style? As they value intellectual rigour and time to reflect – progressing in a thoughtful and considered way – they can sometimes appear counter-cultural in a fast-paced environment where there's an ethos of 'just do it!'. They need to ensure that their approach fits with different organizational cultures.

In a mechanistic organization it is important that any 'blue sky' thinking done by the Thoughtful Architect is grounded in reality. Therefore the patterns and connections that the Thoughtful Architect might see in the internal and external environments, sometimes grasped on a hunch, or through intuition, need to be underpinned by a rigorous problem-solving and decision-making process. Any overarching vision and high-level strategy needs to be almost mechanically linked into sets of cascading objectives. The 'balanced scorecard' is an ideal way of doing this. From the high-level creation of strategy maps, aims and objectives are operationalized into a clear set of interdependent measures.

In a political organization the Thoughtful Architect needs to pay attention to coalitions and allegiances and to individual agendas. These need to be factored into the grand plan or motivating vision, and the different and disparate stakeholders need to understand the part that they will play and the benefits that they will share. The Thoughtful Architect can adopt the role of being the 'Mister Big' behind the scenes, talking to people and providing direction. The task is to establish credentials and credibility and set out the grand scheme of things. The Thoughtful Architect does this by using political skills and stakeholder identification, analysis and management tools. This means thinking through the relationship and importance level of key stakeholders and then developing strategies to work with people accordingly.

In a messy or fluid culture, where the complexity of the internal or external environment suggests that a carefully thought through and planned approach will be redundant before it's implemented, the Thoughtful Architect has to make considerable adjustments to this role. One of the characteristics of the Thoughtful Architect is to consider things and then make a decision to implement a well-formed plan. The messy or fluid environment doesn't allow for this, so they may have to carefully put one or two things in place to influence the organization to start moving in the right direction. In some ways it's a 'tweaking' role.

Thoughtful Architects are great assets in adaptive, changing environments. They can spot what's on the horizon and make sense of it and then look at the internal characteristics of the organization. Then they map out possible strategies to deal with the challenges. The fact that Thoughtful Architects naturally see things from a range of perspectives allows them to generate a number of possible future scenarios with which the organization might be confronted. These leaders can then think through the alternative actions, strategies and tactics which need to be enacted.

EXAMPLES OF THOUGHTFUL ARCHITECTS

George Soros, the billionaire financier and philanthropist, is a Thoughtful Architect. He is best known for his ability to make money from his strategic understanding of the world's financial markets. In order to survive during the post-war period of chaos in Europe he had to use all of his imagination and ingenuity. He grew to be a successful stockbroker through always anticipating the changes in the finance markets. He was able to out-manoeuvre the conventional European financiers, using his imagination and power of logical thought in equal measure to understand the nature of markets and capitalize on that knowledge.

Former US Federal Reserve Chairman Paul Volcker wrote in the foreword of Soros' book *The Alchemy of Finance*: 'George Soros has made his mark as an enormously successful speculator, wise enough to largely withdraw when still way ahead of the game. The bulk of his enormous winnings is now devoted to encouraging transitional and emerging nations to become "open societies", open not only in the sense of freedom of commerce but tolerant of new ideas and different modes of thinking and behavior.'

However, although his power as a Thoughtful Architect is held in awe by many, his goals are often questioned by others. Critics have argued that his philanthropic spending is a smoke screen for empire building. Some say that in post-Communist Russia, Soros' contradictory goals of philanthropist, politician and profiteer became entangled as he had a little too much influence over the Russians. He and Harvard economist Jeffrey Sachs were said to have persuaded Russia to administer 'shock therapy' to the Russian economy. The resulting chaos opened up investment opportunities which some say benefited Soros in the long run.

In 2007, Gordon Brown became prime minister of the UK. He has a first-class degree and a PhD from Edinburgh University, and is said by many to be 'nothing if not complicated'. He is an ideas man; a Thoughtful Architect. As chancellor, Brown was feted for having secured the UK's economic stability and for ensuring the country's strong economic performance. Ex-prime minister Tony Blair has described him as 'brilliant' and a 'tremendous asset to the country'.

Gordon Brown seems to be the antithesis of Tony Blair's charismatic approach and quick-fire policies. He is pragmatic and hard working, often requiring more time and energy to think things through before announcing a new policy than Blair did. He is more inclined to lead by explaining ideas and designs than by the deliberate use of energizing language.

He has other Thoughtful Architect traits, such as always being open to new information and other approaches. Damian Hughes, founder of innovative consultancy and training business www.liquidthinker.com, was quoted as saying:

> Gordon Brown recently declared that one feature of his leadership will be 'a commitment to listen to the people'. Don't dismiss this as mere hot air. A friend of mine, who studied with Brown at Edinburgh, once received a phone call from him in response to a letter he had written complaining about a decision taken in one of his budgets. Brown admitted that he had been unaware of the practical impact it would have on small businesses and vowed to investigate. The legislation was subsequently amended.

One head teacher that we worked with is a successful Thoughtful Architect. She was appointed as the new head of a primary school that was suffering from falling morale and a rather controlling culture. The previous head and the chair of governors had become in the habit of giving direction and others had become in the habit of following. She was very clear about how she saw things changing, but her challenge was to get others to take responsibility for helping her get there. She had a well-thought-through plan for how to do this, and she was completely aware of the different and sometimes competing interests amongst the stakeholders.

How did she approach this? Initially she constructed a mental roadmap of the process of organizational change. This was something she did alone. Then her first key step was to create a leadership team, and to start to shift each senior staff member's mindset from simply managing the school to thinking about contributing to the vision and culture of this living community.

The initial visioning process was purposefully led by the head. She began by explicitly seeking the ideas of senior staff, and over time others became involved and central control was gradually relinquished. Staff began to have a greater say, as did the parents who, through a newly revitalized parents forum, were also included. The pupils themselves were encouraged to set up a school's council and become 'associate governors'. This had all been part of her grand design, but she worked slowly and thoughtfully at enabling others to make it come alive.

Another Thoughtful Architect we know is the director of a key service in a large county council. He took over as Director when the county council's external rating was very low, and his directorate was struggling with many of its key performance measures. Through intense conversations with trusted, experienced colleagues, council members and potential external partners, he began to craft a vision of how this directorate could be restructured and realigned to serve the community much more effectively. This new vision outlined how they would be working in a completely new way that truly engaged local partners, involved the users themselves, and worked alongside the myriad voluntary organizations already thriving in the area, generating new ideas and new social enterprises.

His first challenge was to revitalize the directorate, which had lost confidence in its own ability to deliver. He embarked on a very difficult restructuring exercise, which was designed to shift the balance of power from the centre to the districts, all the time having to ensure that he had enough contact with the top 100 managers to explain the vision, strategy, operating structure and end-goals. He was also very clear about the kind of culture he wanted, because performance information and financial controls had not been securely in place when he arrived, and he really needed to engage people in tackling this.

We noticed that each time he spoke to small or large groups of staff or managers, there was an incredible feeling of fog lifting; of clarity and relief. He had the ability to make the complex simple, and the patience to say things again and again, still embracing new information and responding to perceived glitches in the design by making a tweak here, or a small alteration there. So he was responsive but consistent, and extremely determined. That helped people through a difficult period of transition and enabled them to experience some really high levels of energy and clarity.

We've already encountered Bill Gates' Edgy Catalyser qualities, but he also exhibits many of the Thoughtful Architect behaviours too. People describe his approach to problem solving and decision making as constructing a model of the problem in his head and then being able to analyse the model bit by bit, looking at the disparate parts and identifying where things don't make sense and where the linkages are with other aspects of the system. He doesn't focus on personalities, but what he describes as the product. That is always the end-goal.

Einstein is another example of the Thoughtful Architect. He said: 'To me it suffices to wonder at these secrets and to attempt humbly to grasp with my mind a mere image of the lofty structure of all that there is.' Einstein had an overarching aim to understand the way things are in the world, and he looked for the underlying structure of things. He had an amazing ability to hold these concepts and structures in his head, and was able to construct a mental model of the way the universe operates which was internally consistent and externally verifiable.

Strangely, Einstein had not done well at school. Initially he worked in the Swiss patent office evaluating patents, identifying where they wouldn't work and correcting the design. This was a great job for a Thoughtful Architect. Einstein was relatively introverted and somewhat detached from the world, coming across as both independent and sometimes arrogant, but always pursuing what he described as the 'never-ending task of reason'.

Part 3

The research

10

What roles do effective leaders use?

OBJECTIVES OF THE RESEARCH

We set out to discover how much these five leadership roles are being used by effective organizational leaders, how independent the use of these five roles is, how people view these roles in terms of their effectiveness, attractiveness as a role model and level of difficulty experienced in mastering the role.

RESEARCH GROUP

In January 2007 we began to invite experienced organizational managers to complete an online questionnaire which formed the basis for our investigation into the five leadership roles, and how they manifest themselves in organizational life. Eighty-three people completed the questionnaire; some online, and some on paper. The questionnaire first attempted to uncover to what degree each of these five leadership roles are used by successful leaders, and how participants see the roles demonstrated within their own leadership work. The results of this first part of the research are covered in this chapter. The second part of the research investigated which leadership roles 'suit' which contexts and is described in Chapter 11.

The population who responded was a mix of public, private and voluntary sector managers with around half of the respondents working in the public sector, 40 per cent in the private sector and 10 per cent in the voluntary sector. The vast majority of respondents live and work in the UK, and a small percentage live and work outside the UK. Seventy per cent of the respondents were male and 30 per cent were female.

We asked people to describe the changes in their current work situation by choosing any number of situations from a range of options. The five most popular selections were:

- need to work with a range of partners and stakeholders – 39%;
- cultural change – 33%;
- working towards a new five-year strategy – 33%;
- complex whole-organization change – 29%;
- restructuring – 25%.

ROLES USED BY EFFECTIVE LEADERS

We invited people to think of two effective organizational leaders, and to analyse the way these leaders operate by telling us how much each leader demonstrates each of the five leadership roles. It's worth mentioning that at least two people declined to fill in the questionnaire because they couldn't think of any leaders that they had known throughout their working lives whom they would describe as effective.

In Figure 10.1, you can see the average proportions in which each leadership role was used by the effective leader described. This was derived by adding up all the proportions given for all the leaders described. It's clear that when all the analyses are added together it looks as if, on average, all five leadership roles are used in equal quantities by successful leaders. Further inspection of the data revealed that 80 per cent of the leaders described by respondents used all the roles to some extent.

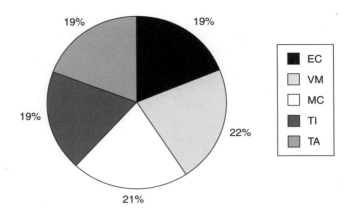

Figure 10.1 Effective leaders. By adding all the scores that participants gave for the strength of use of each role by successful leaders they know, we can see overall that leaders use the roles in almost equal proportion

We wanted to identify any particular leadership patterns; for instance, is there a specific combination of roles that appears to work well in a specific situation? We noticed that leaders of successful turnarounds seem to use the Measured Connector roles a little less than they use the other four roles, whilst leaders of successful complex whole-organization change use the Measured Connector role more than the other roles. No other obvious patterns emerged, indicating that combinations of roles appear to work well in all sorts of situations.

The spread of use of different roles is interesting (see Table 10.1). At least 98 per cent of all successful leaders described in the survey use the Measured Connector role to some extent, making this role appear to be an absolute requirement for leaders to master.

The Visionary Motivator role was also extremely widely used, slightly more so than the Measured Connector role. Nearly 30 per cent of the successful leaders described use the Visionary Motivator role a great deal, with only 15 per cent using any one of the other roles a great deal. It appears that the Visionary Motivator role is one that can be used successfully in large quantities, and is less likely to be used (or spotted?) in small quantities. Perhaps this role can make up for inadequacies in the other roles.

Table 10.1   The spread of use of the different leadership roles – percentage of total number of leaders described using each role in the various different strengths

	Never (1)	Little (2)	Some-what (3)	Much (4)	A great deal (5)	**Weighted average use of each role**
Edgy Catalyser	8%	23%	31%	23%	15%	**19%**
Visionary Motivator	3%	13%	28%	29%	27%	**22%**
Measured Connector	2%	19%	28%	37%	14%	**21%**
Tenacious Implementer	4%	25%	30%	26%	15%	**19%**
Thoughtful Architect	4%	21%	31%	29%	15%	**19%**

The most often ignored, or missing, role was the Edgy Catalyser. Eight per cent of the leaders described didn't use the Edgy Catalyser role at all. The next most absent roles were the Thoughtful Architect and Tenacious Implementer roles, neither of which is used by 4 per cent of the leaders described.

Was there more information to glean about the strength of usage of each role? Only 38 per cent of the leaders described in the survey appeared to be using the Edgy Catalyser role either 'much' or a 'great deal', compared to 56 per cent using the Visionary Motivator role and 51 per cent using the Measured Connector role either 'much' or a 'great deal'. This might indicate that the Edgy Catalyser role is best used in slightly smaller doses, as are the Tenacious Implementer and Thoughtful Architect roles.

ARE THE ROLES INDEPENDENT OF EACH OTHER?

We looked for correlations between the use of all five roles to see whether the use of one gets in the way of the use of another, or if two roles appear to work well hand in hand. This analysis would also tell us if the roles we have proposed are in some way overlapping.

Table 10.2 shows the correlations found between the use of different roles. The correlations that are starred once are low-, and those starred twice are medium-level correlations (according to Cohen (1988)). There were no strong correlations identified in the data collected. Experienced statisticians tell us that only the medium-level correlations are of any real significance, although the other lower correlations are interesting and worth commenting on.

Table 10.2   Correlations between the roles. * = low correlation, ** = medium level correlation. [No star = no correlation]

	Edgy Catalyser	Visionary Motivator	Measured Connector	Tenacious Implementer	Thoughtful Architect
Edgy Catalyser		0.18 *	−0.08	0.373 **	−0.27 *
Visionary Motivator			−0.13 *	0.07	−0.089
Measured Connector				−0.11 *	0.19 *
Tenacious Implementer					0.09
Thoughtful Architect					

The most significant correlation is between the Edgy Catalyser and the Tenacious Implementer role. This is a medium-level positive correlation, which implies that there might be a connection of some sort between the levels of use of these roles. This means that if a leader is a heavy user of the Tenacious Implementer role, it is quite likely that he or she will also be a heavy user of the Edgy Catalyser role, and vice versa. Likewise, if a leader doesn't use the Tenacious Implementer role very much, it is quite likely that he or she does not use the Edgy Catalyser very much either, and vice versa.

It could be that the Edgy Catalyser and Tenacious Implementer roles are overlapping, or maybe they simply work together well. Both are associated with a sense of urgency and a high level of direction, which could be the link. Some might argue that the two roles could be combined. However, we believe that it's important to distinguish the Edgy Catalyser role as we have seen careful use of this role making a big difference to organizational change efforts, and yet the key behaviours associated with it are missing from many management competence lists.

A low positive correlation exists between the Edgy Catalyser and the Visionary Motivator roles, implying that there might be a slight connection between the levels of use of these roles. This may be to do with energy levels. The Visionary Motivator and the Edgy Catalyser are more extroverted forms of leading, and require energy to be displayed, so it's possible that leaders who can master one role might find it easier to master the other.

Likewise the Measured Connector and Thoughtful Architect roles have a low positive correlation, which implies that there is a slight connection between levels of use of these two roles in any one leader. This may be because they are both calmer, less interventionist ways of operating.

The Measured Connector and the Tenacious Implementer roles are slightly negatively correlated, which means that if a leader is a heavy user of one, it is likely that he or she is a low user of the other. This could be because the Measured Connector role is about divergence. It involves opening up discussions and involving people. The Tenacious Implementer is by contrast a convergent role in which the leader encourages people to follow the agreed plan and complete tasks on time. One can imagine that doing both would take some juggling. The Tenacious Implementer role seems to be focused on moving things forward in a very purposeful, linear way whereas the Measured Connector role is ensuring that the linkages are made across the whole organization and beyond in a more networked or spatial way.

The Edgy Catalyser and the Thoughtful Architect are also slightly negatively correlated. Again, this means that if a leader is a heavy user of one it is likely that he or she is a low user of the other. This makes some sense, as these roles are quite different in nature. The Edgy Catalyser points out problems and raises issues with people very directly, whereas the Thoughtful Architect is more inclined to find a solution to something off-line and tackle issues in a more considered way. This might be why use of the Edgy Catalyser role doesn't sit very easily with the use of the Thoughtful Architect role and vice versa. They seem opposite in nature.

None of the correlations that arose from our research were high, which indicates that the five roles are reasonably independent from each other. This suggests confirmation of our belief that each of the five roles can be used independently, and developed independently. This also suggests that each role is likely to have a different use, and therefore a different organizational effect.

WHAT TYPE OF LEADER ARE YOU?

Everyone who completed the questionnaire has been a manager within organizations at some point in their career. We asked them to choose which one of the roles was most like them as a leader or manager (see Figure 10.2). The most popular selection was Measured Connector. Nearly half of those asked said they operated most frequently as a Measured Connector; 26 per cent as Visionary Motivator; 18 per cent as Thoughtful Architect; and only 8 per cent as Edgy Catalyser and 6 per cent as Tenacious Implementer.

Was this as we expected? Maybe the Measured Connector is the most frequently found role in our respondents because it is the most prevalent managerial profile in today's organizations. Or perhaps it's the most natural profile for the type of population that is willing to fill

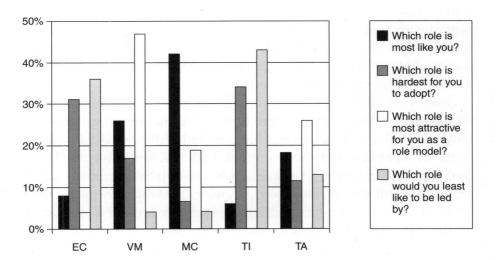

Figure 10.2   Questions about the participants as leaders – 77 respondents answered these questions

in such questionnaires! The role is calm, unhurried, but purposeful and focuses on people and connections between them. The least prevalent roles in our respondent population were the Tenacious Implementer and Edgy Catalyser roles, which are by contrast more directive and task-focused in approach; more reminiscent of the traditional command and control manager. As we had asked people to select only one role, it's possible that the Tenacious Implementer and Edgy Catalyser roles are used by respondents, but just less frequently.

We wonder whether organizations have a natural limit on the uptake of the Edgy Catalyser and Tenacious Implementer roles. Perhaps organizations which have too many people performing these roles develop disconnected and unsupportive cultures, lacking in connectivity or sense of purpose, or any real overarching thought processes.

WHICH OF THE FIVE ROLES DO YOU FIND HARDEST TO ADOPT?

We then asked people which roles were hardest for them to adopt (see Figure 10.2). The Edgy Catalyser and the Tenacious Implementer came joint top of the list. Both of these roles were selected by around 30 per cent of the participants as the hardest roles to adopt. Seventeen per cent of participants named the Visionary Motivator role as the hardest to adopt. The Measured Connector was selected by only 6 per cent and the Thoughtful Architect by 12 per cent. These last two roles seem much easier for most people to access.

Given that all five roles appear to be required for successful leadership, it is intriguing to discover that two of the roles that are regularly used by successful leaders seem to be hard for one-third of the leadership population to access. What might this mean for the development of successful leaders? Much leadership development today focuses on influencing skills and strategic thinking, which are both areas of skill that are contained within the more accessible roles such as the Measured Connector and the Thoughtful Architect. This research would indicate that many leaders also need to learn how to manage and direct complex projects, how to move into and handle difficult situations and how to take an energizing, motivational leadership role. Do we sometimes pay attention to the wrong areas?

What does this say about traditional leadership development routes? The MBA has become a very popular and well-respected route for leaders to develop themselves. MBAs tend to provide theory, research, real-life projects and case studies for students to reflect on. This approach is most aligned with the Thoughtful Architect role which only 12 per cent of the participants in our survey experienced as hard to access. MBAs often concentrate on developing strategic thinking, which can be a very powerful tool for analysing market trends and being creative and flexible in one's mastery of the future. Strategic planning, business process re-engineering, organizational redesign, financial analysis, mergers and acquisitions; these are all Thoughtful Architect approaches to organizational change, heavily supported by MBA research and teaching. However, the success rate of these approaches in developing rounded leaders might be limited if the leader lacks the ability to step into the other four leadership roles. Organizations that have too many Thoughtful Architects may lack connectivity and sense of purpose; be de-energized and lack engagement; lack the ability to deal healthily with conflict; and be less able when it comes to being productive and delivering on target.

We wanted to investigate the relationship between the participant's natural role and the role he or she found hardest to access. See Figure 10.3 for this data. On close inspection of the data it appears that the hardest role for Visionary Motivators to perform is the Tenacious Implementer role, while the hardest role for Tenacious Implementers to perform is the Visionary Motivator role. Perhaps these roles are somehow opposites; the Visionary Motivator works with others to create an attractive future state while the Tenacious Implementer is constantly looking to see what's not being done to reach an already agreed set of deliverables. They are very different approaches to leading, although it's possible to see how a project or change initiative might require both roles to be present in the leadership team.

Thoughtful Architects tend to find the Edgy Catalyser role the most difficult to access, whereas the Edgy Catalysers in our questionnaire found a variety of roles hard to access. Measured Connectors tend to find the Edgy Catalyser and Visionary Motivator roles most difficult to access.

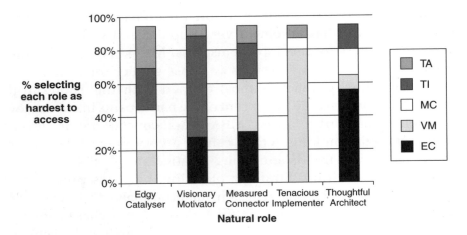

Figure 10.3   Each respondent selected a role that was most like them, which we have called the 'natural role'. This graph shows the relationship between natural role and hardest role to access

WHICH OF THE FIVE ROLES IS MOST ATTRACTIVE AS A ROLE MODEL?

The Visionary Motivator was selected by respondents as the most attractive role model (Figure 10.2). This role was chosen by 47 per cent of participants. The very nature of the Visionary Motivator role is to energize and motivate people, so it's not surprising that in the UK and US contexts, it provides a very attractive role model for nearly half of those asked. We wonder whether this role is so popular, or even so respected, in other populations or cultures. Our experience of working with Malaysian and Indian companies is that senior figures are more likely to occupy Thoughtful Architect roles, or perhaps to use a less extraverted version of the Visionary Motivator role.

The next most attractive role model for our respondents was the Thoughtful Architect, selected by 26 per cent. What is interesting is that stereotypically leaders are often seen as action-oriented, so perhaps it comes as a welcome surprise to see that over a quarter of people valued this role so highly. We imagine that there is some kudos or prestige associated with the Thoughtful Architect role. Perhaps it is linked with a high IQ or a well-developed analytical brain, which we value highly in the UK and the United States. Or perhaps there is a real belief that cognitive, strategic, off-line thinking will solve organizational issues and enable survival.

The Measured Connector was selected as the next most attractive. It was chosen by 18 per cent of participants. However, the Edgy Catalyser and Tenacious Implementer roles were seen as the most attractive role models by only 4 per cent of participants apiece. It's possible that leaders are influenced in their choice of role model by popular leadership literature and by models purveyed by leadership training courses. Perhaps they are also influenced by what they notice is lacking in their own organizations. As respondents themselves appear to recognize that all five roles are being used by successful leaders, it's curious to note that their choices of role model don't appear to reflect this spread. Perhaps this is more of a subjective choice, based on current myths of what a leader 'should' be like, such as those who are strongly promoted as successful leaders like Richard Branson or Steve Jobs. The Edgy Catalyser perhaps is the role which is least likely to win friends and most likely to need an emotional resilience, if not a thick skin! The Tenacious Implementer on the other hand may be associated with the more prosaic and potentially dull aspects of leadership; the project management side of change, although it is nonetheless critical to successful leadership.

We also looked through the data to see whether there were any patterns that emerged from looking at the relationship between an individual's natural role and the role they chose as a role model. See Figure 10.4 for this data. We were intrigued to find that 56 per cent of the Visionary Motivators found Visionary Motivators most attractive as a role model. Only 28 per cent of the Visionary Motivators found Thoughtful Architects attractive role models and 16 per cent found Measured Connectors attractive. Is the Visionary Motivator a narcissistic role perhaps, or just self-sufficient?

We also found that 75 per cent of the Thoughtful Architects completing the survey found the Visionary Motivator role the most attractive as a role model, with only a small interest in the Measured Connector and Tenacious Implementer roles. Around a third of the natural Measured Connectors found the Visionary Motivator the most attractive and a third found the Thoughtful Architect role the most

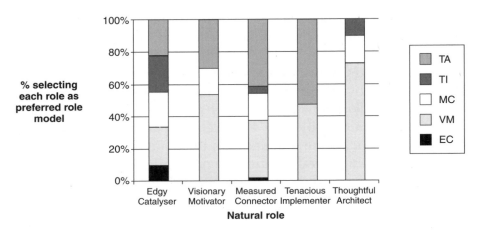

Figure 10.4 Each respondent selected a role that was most like them, which we have called the 'natural role'. This graph shows the relationship between natural role and most preferred role model

attractive. Only 15 per cent of all natural Measured Connectors that participated found the Measured Connector the most attractive role.

Tenacious Implementers were evenly split between admiring the Visionary Motivators and the Thoughtful Architects, whereas Edgy Catalysers admired all the different roles to some extent. Maybe Tenacious Implementers realize that to do their roles really well, they also need to incorporate some of the Visionary Motivator Role and the Thoughtful Architect role. Note that the Edgy Catalyser role was the least attractive role model.

WHICH OF THE ROLES
WOULD YOU LEAST LIKE TO BE LED BY?

When participants were asked which roles they would least like to be led by, the Tenacious Implementer came top at 43 per cent, with the Edgy Catalyser a close second at 36 per cent (see Figure 10.2). The Thoughtful Architect was third in the list, with 13 per cent of those asked naming this role as the one they would least like to be led by. This suggests that the Tenacious Implementer and Edgy Catalyser roles are less likely to meet the support needs of their staff when used in isolation from the other available leadership roles. The Visionary Motivator and Measured Connector roles are more likely to provide supportive, steady relationships for people.

Again, some patterns emerged here. Nearly half of all the Measured Connectors didn't want to be led by Edgy Catalysers. Eighty per cent of the Edgy Catalysers didn't want to be led by Tenacious Implementers and two-thirds of the Visionary Motivators felt the same way. Most Thoughtful Architects don't like to be led by Tenacious Implementers or Edgy Catalysers.

WHICH ARE THE MOST AND LEAST PREVALENT STYLES IN YOUR ORGANIZATION?

Figure 10.5 illustrates the responses to the questions we asked about the most and least prevalent styles used within participants' organizations. The Tenacious Implementer role is the most frequently observed style, with the Edgy Catalyser a close second. Maybe this result reflects the level of urgency and haste present in many organizations, with much chasing of actions and kicking-off of new projects. In our experience, a great deal of this activity is ineffective because the projects tackle surface issues rather than deeper systemic issues, usually because they are conceived too quickly and without the use of a Thoughtful

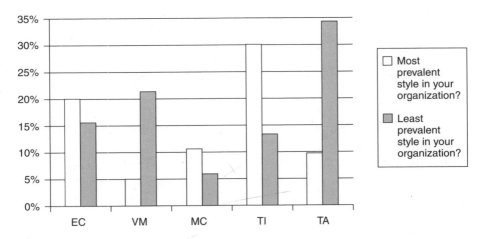

Figure 10.5 Use of styles in participants' organizations

Architect. In a high-pressure, delivery-conscious environment, Thoughtful Architects can be seen as slow and laboured; too focused on details, or problems. However, sometimes that is what is needed.

Least frequently observed styles are the Thoughtful Architect and the Visionary Motivator. We often hear staff yearning for vision from senior managers, with an accompanying yearning to have this backed up with sound rationale. Sometimes leaders are so busy taking responsibility for everything (and becoming a bottleneck) that they have no time left for crafting a well-thought-through vision that takes an organization into the future.

CONCLUSIONS

The five leadership roles appear to be equally significant when we analyse what effective leaders do.

The Measured Connector role is successful in achieving complex whole organizational change, but less useful for organizational turnarounds.

The Visionary Motivator and Measured Connector roles are the most widely used by successful leaders.

The most likely roles to be missing from a successful leader's repertoire are the Edgy Catalyser, the Tenacious Implementer and Thoughtful Architect roles.

The Edgy Catalyser, Tenacious Implementer and Thoughtful Architect roles are more likely to be used by successful leaders to a lesser degree than Measured Connector or Visionary Motivator roles.

There appears to be a connection between the strength of use of the Edgy Catalyser and Tenacious Implementer roles. In some sense, they go together.

Conversely, there appears to be an inverse correlation between the use of the Edgy Catalyser and Thoughtful Architect roles. As one is used more, so the other is used less.

Nearly half of the leaders in our survey classed themselves as most like the Measured Connector role in their leadership approach. This was the most popular choice. The least popular choice was Tenacious Implementer.

The Edgy Catalyser and Tenacious Implementer roles seem to be the hardest for our population to adopt, with the Visionary Motivator role the third hardest. This may have implications for leadership development, which tends to focus on strategic thinking and influencing skills and is therefore not tackling the more challenging areas.

Tenacious Implementers tend to find the Visionary Motivator role hard to access, and vice versa. These roles have very different skills and a very different approach underpinning them, although a combination of the two roles might form a very powerful leadership team.

Thoughtful Architects tend to find the Edgy Catalyser role hard to access.

Nearly half the leaders asked said they found the Visionary Motivator to be the most attractive role model. This was by far the most popular role model, followed by the Thoughtful Architect role, selected by only a quarter of respondents.

Tenacious Implementers and Edgy Catalysers do not make good bosses, unless they are tempered by the use of other contrasting roles.

The Tenacious Implementer and Edgy Catalyser roles are the most commonly observed roles in organizational life. These roles are presumably not always being used successfully as we know that successful leaders on average use all five roles in equal measure.

The least commonly observed roles in organizational life are the Thoughtful Architect and Visionary Motivator roles.

11

Which roles are needed when?

Which roles work in which situations? We invited our research participants to use their organizational wisdom to select the roles they thought would be most effective in a range of contexts. We wanted to find out if different leadership roles, or combinations of roles, matched up to any particular contexts. This type of insight could enable leadership teams to be more choiceful about which leadership roles need to be carried out by team members, for example to progress a particular type of change initiative. This research might also help shed some light on the selection, recruitment and development of leaders, in the sense that it might be more desirable to recruit a leader who excels in one type of role if you are recruiting into a particular context. Our questionnaire therefore asked people to select the one or two leadership roles that they thought would work best in each of a range of organizational contexts.

The summary of results appears in Figure 11.1.

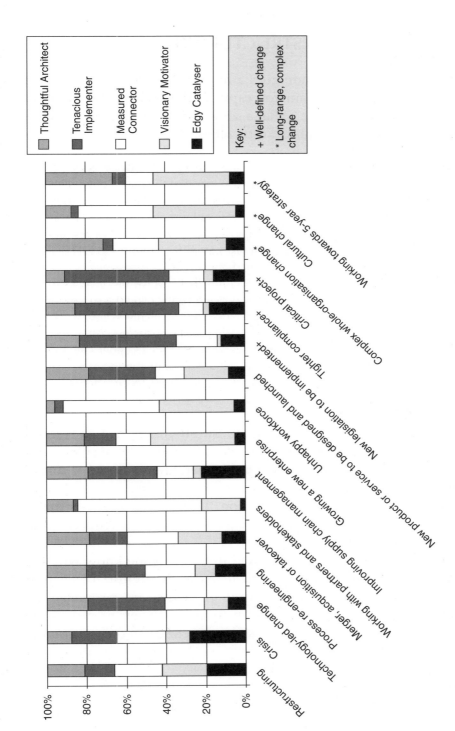

Figure 11.1 Roles participants felt were most important for leaders to adopt in various organizational situations

RESTRUCTURING

When an organization undergoes a major restructuring, it can be a painful exercise. Esther Cameron captures the problematic nature of restructuring in her article 'What a song and dance' (*Guardian*, 2007). This short extract highlights the difficulties:

> [restructuring] is a huge drain on executive energy, takes twice as long as you think to complete and is a costly disruption to the dance of working life. When a major restructuring happens, many fundamental partnerships need to be rebuilt from scratch. One senior project manager I know didn't have the stomach for his employer's merry-go-round of restructurings. He walked out in disgust. 'It takes around 18 months to get back to normal after a restructuring. We had one a year.'
>
> It's not all bad news. Small restructures that involve tiny tweaks to people's jobs often work well. Surrey police recently piloted a successful scheme to redirect detective constables' time to highly skilled work, resulting in three times as many crimes being dealt with for less cost. Larger restructures can work too, as long as everyone has time to understand the rationale and get involved in the redesign. But given the business as usual targets that exist in almost every sector, it's hard to see how real involvement can happen without bucketfuls of backfill.

A quarter of all those completing our questionnaire named restructuring as one of the top change priorities for their organization right now. It's a very common context to be operating in. So what sort of leadership is required for a restructuring process to deliver sustainable gains for the organization? Our survey suggests that a balanced leadership approach is required, with contributions from every one of the five roles.

The Edgy Catalyser role is needed to let everyone know why the restructure is happening, and to feel the discomfort of current problems. Sometimes restructuring processes are provoked by financial problems, other times by an audit or a big event such as the loss of a big customer. Less successful restructures, in our experience, seem to happen in a cloud of mystery, without any clear rationale or existing problem being outlined.

The Visionary Motivator role is needed to begin to engage people in the future. Restructurings are tough to get through because they often have to be drawn-out processes if the leadership want to be seen to be fair and above board. It's a good idea to make sure that people know that once it's all over, a hopeful future will begin to emerge. The Measured Connector role is especially important once the new structure is in place because new relationships and a sense of purpose are both extremely important to sustained success. New connections have to be established and new goals have to be agreed.

During the restructure the Tenacious Implementer is a key role to ensure that plans are doable and deadlines are achieved. Restructurings that incorporate repeated delays take a lot of performance energy out of an organizational system; people need to talk to each other over the water cooler to cope with the uncertainty. This unsteadiness often interferes with even the most dedicated individual's productivity.

The Thoughtful Architect is needed to think through and explain any new processes or ways of working. This leadership role is often undervalued because Thoughtful Architects don't operate at top speed, and may be comfortable with a level of complexity that leaves others feeling confused or anxious. Nonetheless, the Thoughtful Architect is vital when thinking through and explaining a new structure, as often people get into the new posts with absolutely no idea how the new organization is 'supposed' to work.

CRISIS

When an organization gets into a crisis it's very often too late to rescue things. However, when an impending crisis is predicted and dealt with before it takes hold, everyone is very grateful. The advance handling of possible crises is a difficult area. It's so hard to know when to act, which trends or patterns to pay attention to, and it's very challenging to know when sticking with something is better than ditching it.

Charles Handy in his book *The Age of Unreason* (1989) referred to the difficulty of knowing when to change tack as the 'Davy's Bar' syndrome:

> The Wicklow Mountains lie outside Dublin, Ireland. It is an area of wild beauty, a place to which as an Irishman born near there, I return as often as I can. It is still a bare and lonely spot, with unmarked roads, and I still get lost.

Once I stopped and asked the way. 'Sure, it's easy,' a local replied, 'just keep going the way you are, straight ahead, and after a while you'll cross a small bridge with Davy's Bar on the far side. You can't miss it!' 'Yes, I've got that,' I said. 'Straight on to Davy's Bar.' 'That's right. Well, half a mile before you get there, turn to your right up the hill.'

His directions seemed so logical that I thanked him and drove off. By the time I realized that the logic made no sense he had disappeared. As I made my way down to Davy's Bar, wondering which of the roads to the right to take, I reflected that he had given me a vivid example of paradox, perhaps even the paradox of our times; by the time you know where you ought to go, it's too late to go there, or more dramatically, if you keep on going the way you are, you will miss the road to the future.

In the questionnaire, our respondents selected the Edgy Catalyser, the Measured Connector and the Tenacious Implementer as the most important leadership roles in (or just before) a crisis. The Edgy Catalyser helps people to recognize that there is actually a crisis, and with any luck this will become an early warning. The Measured Connector encourages connectivity between important parts of the organization so that responses don't become disjointed, and the Tenacious Implementer urges everyone to stick to the plan for getting out of the mess.

Perhaps the Visionary Motivator and Thoughtful Architect roles are too long range in focus to be useful in a crisis. It's worth adding that many organizations behave as if they are in crisis when they aren't. Signs of this are a great deal of rushing and busy-ness, with a long list of urgent projects and too many people getting involved when something goes wrong. In these organizations, the use of the Visionary Motivator and Thoughtful Architect roles can be extremely beneficial in alleviating this short-termist trap.

TECHNOLOGY-LED CHANGE

Changes that involve the roll-out of new technology can look at first glance to be much more straightforward than they really are. The complexity of this endeavour increases by a factor of 10 if there is any opportunity for tailoring or option-selection by users. Received wisdom on the success of technology-led change is that leaders need to be firm about implementation and roll-out milestones, and how much 'wriggle room' there is for those in receipt of the technology to have it implemented differently.

Our respondents believe that the key leadership roles to use for this sort of change process are the Tenacious Implementer, the Measured Connector and the Thoughtful Architect. Perhaps the Measured Connector role becomes increasingly important the more complex the technology is, and the more cross-functional its implications.

The Edgy Catalyser and Visionary Motivator roles were seen as less important by the majority of correspondents, perhaps because technology-led change is usually presented as a fait accompli, and that creates discomfort in itself. As far as vision is concerned, when it comes to technology, perhaps people would rather have the facts than the possibilities, so that they can begin to prepare for its arrival.

PROCESS RE-ENGINEERING

Process re-engineering comes in many forms, from the top-down expert-led change to the more involving front-line-initiated 'lean' approaches. The Measured Connector and Tenacious Implementer roles were selected as most important for leading this type of work.

This is confirmed by recent research by consultancies operating in this field showing that non-directive, more involving leadership approaches are the most successful when leading process re-engineering teams. Those managers and staff on the ground need to be trusted to come up with ideas and generate solutions to the challenges that process engineering generates.

Our survey indicated that the Tenacious Implementer, Measured Connector and Thoughtful Architect roles are the most important in this type of context, with the Tenacious Implementer coming out as a clear winner. Lack of committed leadership and lack of resources are often blamed for the failure of business process re-engineering (BPR) initiatives. Thus a Tenacious Implementer's tendency to establish a workable plan and then stick to it is vital to successful re-engineering efforts.

Measured Connectors provide the cross-functional leadership that might be needed to ensure that a purposeful, outcomes-oriented re-engineering effort emerges that truly involves people who work on processes that don't normally intertwine. Thoughtful Architects will be useful to provide some of the trickier thinking to design new ways of working and to see how all this fits into the organization's future plans.

Visionary Motivators and Edgy Catalysers are seen as less useful roles in this context. As process re-engineering is usually considered to be a planned activity, the Edgy Catalyser isn't necessary for generating the discomfort that causes action to take place. Visionary Motivators are perhaps seen as less useful because it's rarely lack of engagement or hope for the future that scuppers this type of process. It's more likely to be lack of support from senior leaders or concern from those taking part that they or others might lose jobs.

MERGER, ACQUISITION OR TAKEOVER

Mergers, acquisitions and takeovers all suffer from a similar root problem when they go wrong. The leadership team fails to sit down and work out what the purpose of the exercise is, and subsequently fails to set out a strategy that leads to meeting this purpose. A list of possible purposes provides a useful checklist. What is the purpose of the merger, acquisition or takeover? The purpose then begins to tell us something about what type of leadership is needed:

- growth;
- synergy;
- diversification;
- integration to achieve economic gains;
- to do a deal, any deal!

Some organizations that are successful acquirers have developed very sophisticated ways of tackling this process so that it is successful and brings sustainable benefits. Ispat Industries Limited was cited by Aiello and Watkins (2000) as having just such an approach:

> Ispat is an international steel making company which successfully pursues long-term acquisition strategies. It is one of the world's largest steel companies and its growth has come almost entirely through a decade-long series of acquisitions.

Ispat's acquisitions are strictly focused. They never go outside of their core business. They have a well-honed due diligence process which they use to learn about the people who are running the company and convince them that joining Ispat gives them an opportunity to grow.

Ispat relies on a team of 12 to 14 professionals to manage its acquisitions. Based in London, the team's members have solid operational backgrounds and have worked together since 1991.

The company works with the potential acquisition's management to develop a five-year business plan that will not only provide an acceptable return on investment but that will chime with Ispat's overall strategy.

The only role that our respondents selected in fairly low proportion was the Edgy Catalyser role, whereas the Visionary Motivator, Measured Connector, Tenacious Implementer and Thoughtful Architect roles are all seen as equally important. It's easy to see that the Visionary Motivator role is useful for engaging new staff, and the Measured Connector role can work on integration and synergy together with establishing a joint sense of purpose. The Tenacious Implementer role enables due diligence to be planned and carried out with efficiency and thoroughness, and the Thoughtful Architect role may be needed to help to think through the connected five-year strategy.

Perhaps the Edgy Catalyser role isn't needed because the big event that provoked the change has already happened. There is already enough discomfort around! Perhaps also one of the primary purposes is to make connections, not spot disconnects.

WORKING WITH PARTNERS AND STAKEHOLDERS

The need to work with a wide range of partners and stakeholders is very high on the agenda for most organizations. In our survey nearly 40 per cent of our respondents said that it was one of the priorities for their organization right now. This need is particularly complex and constantly shifting for those who work in the public sector in the UK. Private sector organizations also need to work within a web of interconnected partnerships to ensue that customers get what they need. Corporate social responsibility agendas and issues of sustainability also mean paying more attention to a range of stakeholders.

Unsurprisingly, the Measured Connector was named by almost all respondents as one of the most important leadership roles to use in this context. Working with stakeholders and partners is not just about getting people together, it's also about jointly arriving at a crisp, clear sense of purpose. The Measured Connector role is perfectly tuned for just this type of role.

The Visionary Motivator and Thoughtful Architect roles came second and third in the list, but a long way behind the Measured Connector, with the Edgy Catalyst and Tenacious Implementers only being selected a couple of times each. Respondents seemed to think that creating discomfort and paying attention to good planning were far less important than establishing a sense of connection. Perhaps it's just that the latter two roles will not work at all without some sound connectivity in place.

IMPROVING SUPPLY CHAIN MANAGEMENT

Supply chain management is about improving the way your organization finds the raw components it needs to make a product or service and deliver it to customers. A key part of this is producing a plan for each supplier which defines metrics and a mechanism for monitoring and improving the relationships.

Unsurprisingly, the Tenacious Implementer role comes top of the list of effective leadership roles. The pitfalls of this type of exercise are all created through poor planning, lack of contingency, workarounds, and lack of clarity with suppliers. The Visionary Motivator role was seen as far less important, selected by only four people. It's interesting to note that a major organizational change such as this can probably be achieved without particular attention to engaging people in the future; it's as if a clear plan and good attention to the task are the main vehicles for the change.

GROWING A NEW ENTERPRISE

The type of leadership that's needed to grow a new enterprise is highly sought after. Entrepreneurs appear to be so much more successful than everyone else in creating wealth for themselves and for others. Research carried out in 2000 shows that entrepreneurs are extremely good at interacting effectively with others, and can adjust well to new situations and people. They are less likely than others to engage in counterfactual thinking (ie asking 'what if that event hadn't happened?' questions, or rewriting the past) but more likely to show overconfidence in their own judgements. This is the 'bounce-back-ability' so often described by football commentators when a team manages to win despite previous dismal failures.

The Visionary Motivator role came out as by far the most important leadership role for leaders in charge of a new enterprise. This is the role with the most positive energy, ability to enthuse and engage, and the will to connect with people beyond the normal humdrum relationships that are available in the business world.

The Edgy Catalyser was seen as the least helpful role, which may be because the challenges of growing a new enterprise are uncomfortable enough without the Edgy Catalyser pointing out what's wrong or what needs fixing.

UNHAPPY WORKFORCE

An unhappy workforce is an unproductive workforce. Some of the possible causes of unhappiness amongst staff in an organization are lack of information about the organization's progress, uncertainty about one's future, lack of reward for work well done or even any pause for celebration, constant criticism from superiors, lack of room for creativity, a depressing or uncomfortable environment, lack of a sense of belonging to a peer group or lack of pride in the organization.

What type of leadership helps to shift this? The Measured Connector and Visionary Motivator roles were selected most frequently by our respondents as the most appropriate leadership roles to adopt when tackling low morale. The Measured Connector helps people to belong to something that has a clear purpose, and to feel connected to others. The Visionary Motivator leads by example, showing energy and enthusiasm for the work and for the people involved.

One CEO we know visits each of the business units in her patch once every three months. When she visits morale shoots up, people feel energized and there's an atmosphere of everyone believing that their work is worthwhile. They want to work hard for this woman. Her use of the Visionary Motivator role is very powerful.

Company staff surveys are popular tools for measuring morale; in fact very often this is the only tool that's recognized as giving credible data. The trouble is that the leadership's response to survey results is often disappointing. In the worst-case scenario, senior managers issue a plan itemizing how each area of deficiency will be met, or, slightly better, they ask team leaders to set various team action points in response to the survey results. Either way, these are remarkably uninspiring responses. It's worth noting that the Tenacious Implementer was chosen by only a very small number of people as the ideal role to take in this situation, indicating that this type of planned and monitored response to issues of morale does not meet the perceived need.

NEW PRODUCT OR SERVICE TO BE DESIGNED AND LAUNCHED

The launch of a new product or service is a stressful business. It's often a struggle to meet deadlines and to maintain quality, and most organizations are very mindful that their performance in both of these areas is vital to maintaining customer confidence.

The Tenacious Implementer was the most frequently selected role, followed by the Thoughtful Architect and the Visionary Motivator. As deadlines and quality are so important when launching a new offer, the Tenacious Implementer's role in keeping things on track is paramount. Visionary Motivators are important for engaging staff and customers in the future, and the Thoughtful Architect makes sure that the product or service is well designed with the future in mind and that the whole thing makes sense and is strategically sound.

NEW LEGISLATION, TIGHTER COMPLIANCE AND CRITICAL PROJECT – WELL-DEFINED CHANGE

All three of these seemingly well-defined changes have a similar profile of leadership roles selected. The Tenacious Implementer is by far the most important role in the eyes of our respondents. For this type of change, plans and details need to be watertight and the resources need to be in place, with the right level of focus on progress and issues along the way. The Edgy Catalyser, Thoughtful Architect and Measured Connector roles are all there, but seen as less important.

The Visionary Motivator role is by far the least important role in this context. This matches our experience with expert project staff such as IT people or engineers. Rational, logical people have a tendency to be suspicious of unsubstantiated vision, and get nervous of overconfidence about a solution or a plan. Perhaps that's why the Visionary Motivator role is not required when it comes to well-defined change programmes with a technical content. What the experts require is a realistic plan, clarity about the aims and a good rationale for doing the work, plus the right resources and, ideally, some scope for learning something new.

COMPLEX WHOLE-ORGANIZATION CHANGE, CULTURAL CHANGE AND WORKING TOWARDS A FIVE-YEAR STRATEGY – LONG-RANGE COMPLEX CHANGE

What leadership roles are required when the organization faces long-range complex changes such as whole-organization change, cultural change or a deliberate attempt to work towards a five-year strategy? The Visionary Motivator role is consistently the most frequently selected role for leading long-range complex change, followed closely by a combination of the Thoughtful Architect and the Measured Connector roles.

Whole-organization change and five-year strategy programmes were seen to need slightly more of the Thoughtful Architect leadership role, whereas cultural change required more of the Measured Connector role.

The Tenacious Implementer and Edgy Catalyser roles were selected far less frequently, which possibly reflects the belief that longer-range change is more emergent and needs less hands-on managing. John Kotter's research into 'Why transformation efforts fail', culminating in his *Harvard Business Review* article (1995), contradicts this view. He points to eight key areas for leaders to focus on to ensure that long-range, complex change really takes root:

- Establish a sense of urgency.

- Form a powerful guiding coalition.

- Create a vision.

- Communicate the vision.

- Empower others to act on the vision.

- Plan for and create short-term wins.

- Consolidate improvements and produce still more change.

- Institutionalize new approaches.

This list appears to imply that Visionary Motivator and Thoughtful Architect roles are useful early on in the change process, with a dash of Edgy Catalyser to give a sense of urgency, and after the vision is all clear, the Tenacious Implementer role takes over.

Conversely, our survey indicates that if strategy, buy-in and connectivity are continuously attended to, then the implementations happen more naturally, without such a need for discomfort or very visible monitoring and controlling leadership.

WELL-DEFINED CHANGE VERSUS LONG-RANGE COMPLEX CHANGE

It's worth noting the very marked difference between the leadership roles required to lead convergent, well-defined change processes such as technology-led roll-outs or supply chain improvement exercises, and the leadership roles required to lead more complex, longer-range changes such as cultural change, or whole-organization transformation, that take years to take hold. See Figure 11.2 for the difference between the two leadership profiles.

Sometimes these types of change become muddled in leaders' minds. A complex change such as a shift in the core purpose of the

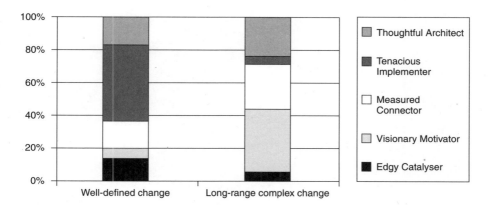

Figure 11.2   The difference between leadership roles selected to match two different contexts: for well-defined change and long-range complex change

organization can get erroneously broken down into falsely simple packages that can then be 'project managed'. This is often a mistake, and misses the complexity and richness of the intended change. We encountered this within a large management consultancy. It needed to shift from taking on only private sector work to doing much more public sector and government work, which promised to be much more profitable. This necessitated a really big change in attitude from employees, who had previously looked down on public sector work. Instead of bringing people together and facing this, the leadership team decided to produce a booklet describing the new company values and circulate it to everyone. This was beautifully project managed, but had absolutely no impact.

Part 4

Expanding your role repertoire

12

Self-assessment

Step 1: For each question in Table 12.1 below, please distribute 12 points amongst the possible responses A–F according to what you would be most likely to do if faced with the situation described. You may allocate anything from 0 to 12 points to each response as long as the total number of points allocated for that question is no more than 12.

Table 12.1 Leadership role questionnaire

No.	Question and responses	Points
1	**The boss wants you to give a presentation at the annual management conference persuading people to get involved in a new business improvement process that your team has been using successfully. Do you:**	
A	Assume it's just not a priority so you put it to the back of your mind until the day before.	
B	Work over the weekend to come up with a careful design for the presentation based on accurate data and a model of the process.	
C	Book time with the boss and ask why he is not promoting this business improvement approach himself at the conference; why is he leaving this to you?	

D	Practise delivering a powerfully persuasive presentation and get feedback from your commercial manager on how you come across.	
E	Invite two members of your team to work up and give the presentation together.	
F	Sketch out some headings and ask one of your team to produce a structured slide-set for you to deliver and to let you have it for a run-through a week before.	
2	**One of the projects that you are responsible for appears to be drifting off schedule. Do you:**	
A	Call a project meeting and enthuse about the importance of the relationship with this specific customer, and let people know how personally disappointed you would be if they were let down by this team.	
B	Talk to everyone involved and then work with the team to analyse what's going wrong, and come up with a new design or plan or structure that solves the problem.	
C	At the next programme board meeting, remind everyone of the importance of keeping to schedules, without mentioning this specifically.	
D	Gather the key people together for a crisis meeting, tell them what concerns you face to face, and ask them for their response. Keep at it until they solve the problem and things are back on track.	
E	Given your ability to manage projects well it's unlikely that you would get into this situation because you have such a sharp eye on progress.	
F	Ask the project leaders to sit down with an expert from another area who has successfully delivered a similar project and take her advice on how to progress.	
3	**There is a major conflict between two of your management team peers which involves endless arguments in meetings and a lack of cooperation with each other about important organizational issues. How do you deal with this?**	
A	Have an off-the-record conversation with Human Resources personnel about how useless these two people are.	

B	Tell them both at the next meeting that you need them to work together more constructively and give examples of where this hasn't happened.	
C	Meet with each individual separately, telling each one how much you value them, and encourage them to make an effort with each other for the sake of the whole organization.	
D	Ask Human Resources to work with you to design and run a conflict resolution process.	
E	Try to help to strengthen the team's sense of purpose and awareness of collective ground-rules by arranging a two-day management team workshop, facilitated by an experienced organizational consultant.	
F	Ask your boss to be more formal about setting actions at management meetings and following these up, so that the two individuals can be managed more carefully.	
4	**Some of your customers say there are some big supply chain issues that you need to attend to urgently. What do you do?**	
A	Kick-off a supply chain improvement project which has as its first phase, a quick investigation and summary of the current issues.	
B	Ask one of your internal change facilitators to organize a meeting to draw out the key issues involving the customers who have strong views, key managers and one or two of your closer and more trusted suppliers.	
C	Through talking to experts in the field, begin to develop a grand design for how the supply chain needs to work to become best in class over the next 5–10 years.	
D	Set up face-to-face meetings with your internal supply management people, and subsequently your suppliers, and let them know how concerned you are and how quickly you need this to be solved.	
E	Copy an article on supply chain difficulties which you came across in a trade magazine to everyone involved.	
F	Begin talking to people one-to-one and in meetings about how excited you are about the possibilities of really improving the supply chain and start floating some ideas about how this could be done and what results you might hope for.	

5	You have just been promoted to Service Manager, taking over a team that is said by senior management to be low performing. How do you handle this?	
A	Pay no attention to the performance information at all and decide that things will improve by themselves now that you're in charge.	
B	Investigate the performance issues and if they seem valid, talk to the individuals or teams concerned, approaching the issues head-on, highlighting what appears to be wrong, how it's viewed by you and senior management and raising the importance of sorting this out.	
C	Implement a rigorous performance management system based on performance indicators and monthly in-depth reports.	
D	Talk to each team leader about how things work at the moment, and begin to picture in your own mind how this service could be managed more strategically and more effectively in the future.	
E	Begin your first team meeting by saying how pleased you are to be leading the team, and talking energetically about performance improvements, and how good that will make you all feel when you get it right over the next few months of working together.	
F	Talk to the previous service manager to see how he or she saw the helps and hindrances to good performance.	
6	One very experienced member of your team is retiring in the next six months and you need to consider how to deal with this situation. Do you:	
A	Encourage the individual to visualize the legacy she would like to leave with the organization and help her to deliver that.	
B	Plan out the transfer of responsibilities to her successor with milestones and checkpoints.	
C	Ask her to work with you to devise the strategy for her area for the next 5–10 years, and possibly stay on as a consultant after the point of retirement.	
D	Don't make a special issue of it – people come and go all the time, and you're confident the next job holder will pick it up.	

E	Ask the individual to spend as much time with one or two specific other people in the team before she goes.	
F	Tell those taking over her role that they need to quickly sort out how to ensure that her experience is captured.	
7	**You and the team have decided that it's time to have an away day together to focus on strategy. Which of these do you typically do?**	
A	Come up with a broad design for the day and then spend some time crafting a talk on your thoughts on future strategy.	
B	Ask Human Resources to put something fun together – and maybe include a strengths/weaknesses/opportunities/threats exercise.	
C	List the content you want to cover and set the agenda.	
D	Ask the team what they would like to cover on the away day and have a decent conversation about it at the next meeting.	
E	Highlight the three issues you are most concerned about and devote the day to cracking these problems with the team.	
F	Talk to your most trusted team member about the key messages you would like to give to the team on the day, and start to practise phrases and keywords that seem to you to say something exciting about the future for this team.	
8	**A key customer has just issued a new guide on product quality which you didn't know was coming. Do you:**	
A	Ask your chief technical officer to go through the new guide and let you know how it differs from your current practice.	
B	Get on the phone to your service managers asking what they know about this new guide, and what they are planning to do about it.	
C	Spend time at your next team meeting discussing this policy in relation to your established good practice – and decide how to deal with any issues arising.	
D	Give everyone a deadline by which time this policy must be implemented and ask everyone to submit a short plan of action.	

E	Copy the guide to everyone with no particular instructions.	
F	Use the new guide to inform a good news story about attention to quality in the next customer bulletin.	
9	**You work in the UK and your counterpart in Germany is using an excellent online tool for tracking sales which you like the look of. Do you:**	
A	Feel quietly envious but decide to say and do nothing.	
B	Ask one of your team to go over to Germany to find out how it all works.	
C	Say pointedly at your next meeting, 'I need this team to be emulating all the good stuff they are doing in Germany. Who will take responsibility for making that happen as soon as possible?'	
D	Ask for the specification of the tool and pore over the design to check that it does what you need.	
E	Visit Germany yourself, decide which element of the tool you need and set a timescale for rolling out the tool in the UK.	
F	Start talking to the team about what you see as the immense possibilities offered by using this tool.	
10	**Your boss is an extremely demanding and highly critical person. How do you deal with this?**	
A	Ensure that you agree targets and review against these so that there is no argument about your achievements.	
B	Try to be as positive as possible about him and to him; try to work out how to push his buttons and what makes him tick.	
C	Maintain a distance and communicate via well-worded e-mails.	
D	Confront him on issues where you believe he is downright wrong and his approach is damaging the work of the team.	
E	Find out how to handle him by talking to people whom you know in common.	
F	Avoid him.	

Step 2: Please fill in Table 12.2 by transposing the scores from Table 12.1, entering them question by question in the table below. Add up the number in each column and fill in the TOTAL row for each of EC, VM etc.

Table 12.2   Leadership roles scoring matrix

		EC		VM		MC		TI		TA		NL
1	C		D		E		F		B		A	
2	D		A		F		E		B		C	
3	B		C		E		F		D		A	
4	D		F		B		A		C		E	
5	B		E		F		C		D		A	
6	F		A		E		B		C		D	
7	E		F		D		C		A		B	
8	B		F		C		D		A		E	
9	C		F		B		E		D		A	
10	D		B		E		A		C		F	
TOTAL												

Step 3: Transfer the totals to Table 12.3 below.

Table 12.3   Leadership roles total scores

Total EC Score =	(Edgy Catalyser)
Total VM Score =	(Visionary Motivator)
Total MC Score =	(Measured Connector)
Total TI Score =	(Tenacious Implementer)
Total TA Score =	(Thoughtful Architect)
Total NL* Score =	(Non-Leadership*: this score indicates when you take a non-leadership role)

Step 4: Analyse your score by circling the range within which your score lies on Table 12.4 below.

A very low score most likely indicates that you need to develop your use of a particular role. A low score may also indicate that you need to develop your use of a particular role.

A medium score indicates that this is a role you visit reasonably frequently. If all your scores are medium (apart from the non-leadership role), you probably have a very balanced leadership style. You might like to play to your strength occasionally instead of being so beautifully even!

A high or very high score may indicate that you are fully proficient in the use of this role. It's also possible that a very high score may indicate that you need to reduce your use of this role, depending on the context in which you are leading.

The exception to all this is the 'Non-Leadership' role, which is there to remind you that some responses to situations are not leadership responses at all. If this score is anything but low or very low, read through the responses and reflect on your non-leadership stance!

Table 12.4   Leadership roles scoring grid – circle your scoring level

Edgy Catalyser	Very low score 0–9	Low score 10–19	Medium score 20–29	High score 30–39	Very high score 40 & above
Visionary Motivator	Very low score 0–9	Low score 10–19	Medium score 20–29	High score 30–39	Very high score 40 & above
Measured Connector	Very low score 0–9	Low score 10–19	Medium score 20–29	High score 30–39	Very high score 40 & above
Tenacious Implementer	Very low score 0–9	Low score 10–19	Medium score 20–29	High score 30–39	Very high score 40 & above
Thoughtful Architect	Very low score 0–9	Low score 10–19	Medium score 20–29	High score 30–39	Very high score 40 & above
Non-Leadership	Very low score 0–9	Low score 10–19	Medium score 20–29	High score 30–39	Very high score 40 & above

13

How to step into a new role

KNOWING YOURSELF

The first thing to realize is that in order to step into a new role, you need to know yourself. This is true for actors as well as leaders. It's important to be able to access all your experiences and talents if you want to expand your ability to perform well in a range of roles. There may be times in the past when you have acted as an Edgy Catalyser and it worked. There may be times when you unexpectedly acted as a Visionary Motivator, and inspired a whole group of people. These experiences are important to recall, understand and draw on.

There are various key questions that it's important to be able to answer about yourself before you even start to develop as a leader such as:

- Who are you?
- What do you stand for?
- What are your natural behaviour patterns?
- How do you think and feel?
- What interests you?

> You need to accept that you are far from a blank sheet.

Psychometrics and 360-degree feedback mechanisms will help, as will simply asking people to tell you what's special about you, what they appreciate about you, what irritates them about you and what they'd like you to do differently. You need to accept that you are far from a blank sheet.

YOUR BEHAVIOUR PATTERNS

The Myers Briggs Type Indicator© is a good way to find out more about who you are. It will tell you how you prefer to take in information and make decisions compared to other people. This will give you a good sense of which activities and ways of working you find easy and enjoyable, and which activities and ways of working are more stressful and draining for you. This sort of questionnaire can now be accessed very easily online, and is a great starting point for increased self-awareness.

KNOWING WHAT YOU ARE ABOUT

What you stand for in the world is important too. Are you pro-market economy, are you anti-war? What's your political stance? Do you believe there's a God? What's important to you? What are you trying to achieve for yourself, your family, your organization, your community? What are your principles of living? The more you know about yourself in this respect, the more self-confident and convincing you will become.

Here's my stand in relation to my work to give you an example:

> I want to devote my working life to enabling a healthy flow of leadership and responsibility-taking in complex organizations. I will work hard to establish open, honest and collaborative partnerships with clients which are underpinned by clear agreements. I strive to treat every assignment as an enquiry, while aiming to be generous with my knowledge and expertise when it's needed.

KNOWING YOUR FLEXIBILITY AND YOUR ASPIRATIONS

When you look through the descriptions of the five leadership roles, you will notice that there are one or two roles which you have already mastered well and which have now become second nature to you. Then you will notice that one or two of the roles are roles that you think you visit from time to time, but you're not very sure how convincing or competent you are in these roles. Finally you will notice that there is at least one role that feels as if it is completely beyond you, or seems to be outside your experience.

We all have a degree of flexibility, and we all have our limits. Bill Gates will never be a Measured Connector, and Sven-Goran Eriksson will never be a Visionary Motivator. There are some roles that are just too far from your natural style to feel possible.

However, our aspirations can increase our flexibility. For instance, I find the Tenacious Implementer role very difficult to do, but if I had aspirations to be a project manager, I might find a way to start to embody the role. It would be hard work, and maybe in the end I would give up and get someone else to do it for me.

CHALLENGING YOUR LIMITING BELIEFS AND AIMING HIGH!

In one sense it's a good idea to know about your limitations, especially those which really cannot be shifted. However, it's also important to challenge your own notion of what's possible. Some of our ideas about limitations are entirely false. For instance, the statements below, made by leaders at the start of a leadership development programme, are unnecessarily limiting:

- 'I can't change the way I am.'

- 'I am someone who doesn't pay attention to time.'

- 'I can't just suddenly become inspirational. I have a monotone voice.'

- 'It's not possible to change your leadership style; it's natural.'

- 'I only like working with highly motivated people.'

- 'I don't believe in making things easy for my staff.'

- 'I am a high-energy manager.'

We spontaneously play a wide variety of roles in life. Imagine yourself attending a presentation given by your boss for you and a group of important clients. Then imagine yourself going to a relaxed Christmas party with your close friends. The way you dress, the way you behave and talk and the way you feel will be completely different. Even your posture and your thought patterns will be different. So already, you have access to a variety of different versions of you, which you can draw on at will.

We are also able to play different roles in relation to different people. If you are working at home one day, tapping away at the computer, and suddenly the doorbell rings, you will project a different version of you depending on who is at the door. If it's a policeman you will act very differently from how you act if it's a confrontational neighbour, an old friend or your mother.

We also have access to other people every day. Normally we focus on how *we* are feeling and thinking about *ourselves* in an interaction, but it's also possible to spend a bit of effort on imagining how the other person is thinking and feeling. If your boss comes into your office and sits down on the chair opposite you, a little slumped, talking about what a terrible day he's had, rubbing his forehead and closing his eyes, you have the possibility of trying to imagine what he's going through instead of feeling annoyed that he's wasting your time. How does it feel to sit like that and say that?

THE POWER OF ROLE PLAYING

In this book we have deliberately described leadership roles rather than leadership competences, and we have equally deliberately encouraged role playing and experimentation rather than skills development. Why is this? What's different about playing a role that goes beyond skills development?

Role playing is the process of *feeling* what it's like to be in a role, rather than studying a specific character's behaviours and learning how to reproduce them. Role playing is a more embodied type of learning which is inner-directed rather than outer-directed. Inner-directed role playing means identifying with a particular character and trusting that the character's actions will arise in the moment. Outer-directed acting means creating an objective representation of what a character would do in a certain situation, and then reproducing that. The latter is a little alienating, and can be rather lifeless. The former is more risky and therefore more stretching so is more likely to result in some real learning.

It's what the Broadway actress, Uta Hagen (*Respect for Acting*, 1973), calls 'really wearing the pants of the character'. This is not just for actors; role playing is a powerful way of learning that children use from a very early age and that adults give up far too easily, most through embarrassment and self-consciousness. The Soviet psychologist Vygotsky (*Mind in Society*, 1978) said: 'In play a child always behaves beyond his average age, above his daily behaviour; in play it's as if he were a head taller than himself.' He saw role playing in children as a natural way for them to develop an understanding of the perceptions and feelings of both others and themselves, thus transitioning them beyond the egocentric stance of the pre-toddler child. Just imagine what adults could gain from this type of experimental activity.

Through attending a wide range of in-company personal skills training courses, most leaders become used to a rather over-prescribed type of role playing that has unwittingly squeezed out the chance of genuine experimentation through offering scripted roles, generous amounts of preparation time and careful feedback; it's all very comfortable but where's the spontaneity, where's the fun and where's the learning edge?

HOW TO GET INTO A NEW ROLE

In the following sections we encourage you to expand your repertoire of roles. First, complete the self-assessment questionnaire in the previous chapter, which will tell you which roles you do most naturally and those which you use less often or not at all.

Start with the roles that are most familiar to you, and then move into the more unfamiliar by stepping into each one in turn. First, rate yourself in the role by answering the 10 questions at the start of the relevant section. This should begin to warm you up into the role. Then go back to Part 2 and read the section entitled 'Inner experience' for the role you have chosen. After that, try out some of the exercises. These work well if you try them out with a group of friends.

HOW TO ACCESS A ROLE

Use your emotional memory to help you to access a particular role. Think of a time when you successfully played the role you want to be, for example Tenacious Implementer. Go back to that time in your mind, remembering where you were, what you were wearing. Recall the look and feel of the place you were in, with all its richness of touch and smell, the weather at the time, the dusty broken Venetian blind flapping on the window, the chipped vase of wilting roses, the smell of a strong coffee on your colleague's breath. Remember what you did and how you did it. Pick on one small but highly significant physical detail of the environment and forever associate that object with the feelings of playing that role on that day. In the future, you will be able to use your memory of the object to access the role you want to step into.

DEVELOP YOUR 'IN THE MOMENT' SPONTANEITY

If you want to use a particular role at work, try warming yourself up into it first. For instance, if I wanted to step into an Edgy Catalyser role at a conference I am facilitating tomorrow, I would warm up by trying to imagine what an Edgy Catalyser would be doing in my world today. I am sitting in my office with the fire on, cosily inhabiting my own quiet corner of the universe. However, I have just received an e-mail from a potential client that's very provoking, and full of potential problems for both me and the client. If I were an Edgy Catalyser, I would quickly compose an e-mail back which highlighted where the proposed solution falls short of our set of agreed outcomes and ask her to fix it.

DEVELOPING THE EDGY CATALYSER IN YOU

Rate yourself as an Edgy Catalyser

Score yourself from 1 to 5 (1 = strongly disagree, 2 = disagree, 3 = agree a little, 4 = agree, 5 strongly agree):

1. I am clear and precise with the facts when I need to argue a point.

2. I don't tend to just let things go if I think they are important.

3. I am recognized for my ability to deal with conflict well.

4. I am courageous when speaking up about a problem that others don't see.

5. I enjoy a robust conversation and encourage my team to give honest feedback.

6. I am good at spotting problems and can quickly see which are important and which are trivial.

7. I am comfortable with the notion that some people don't like me, but I can still work with these people without that getting in the way.

8. I can show my disappointment or my sense of urgency in a way that affects people without getting angry or aggressive.

9. I can juggle a number of conflicts without getting stressed.

10. I am able to enlist support from others when the situation demands it.

Check these scores with your colleagues – especially the people you manage.

Score analysis

If you score more than 30 then you are well on the way to mastering the Edgy Catalyser role. If you score less than 25, try practising the role using the exercises listed below. If you score less than 20, you may have to concede defeat and ensure that you include an Edgy Catalyser on your leadership team.

Practising the role

Exercise 1

Imagine you are in a restaurant having a meal with a friend. The food you have in front of you is lukewarm, and the wine tastes of vinegar. Run a role play with two others in which you, the customer, point out the problem in a respectful but frank and direct way, without telling anyone what to do, but making it clear that you would like something done. The others in the role play can play their roles according to your instructions. For example, one can be the disinterested waiter, and the other your embarrassed dining partner. Give them roles which you might find difficult to deal with.

Debrief afterwards with each other – discussing how they experienced your Edgy Catalyser approach – and reflect on what you found easy/difficult to do. You could try the role play again, but this time, allow yourself to exaggerate your role and even say things you would never say in reality. Discuss the experiment afterwards and talk about what it means for your quest to become an Edgy Catalyser.

Exercise 2

Think of a difficult and important issue at work which no one is speaking up about and which you care about deeply. Maybe your team is not working well together, or one of the computer systems you are using is hopelessly slow or the management team is dysfunctional. List and then practise different ways of drawing people's attention to the problem. Start with straightforward approaches, and then move into more adventurous ways of communicating. Review the list for ideas that might really work.

Try them out if you dare; less risky ones first please! Make notes on what works, and prepare for the discomfort.

Exercise 3

Practise being an Edgy Catalyser with yourself. Identify an issue in your work or personal life that you feel needs attention. Find a quiet room with two chairs. Ask yourself a series of questions from chair one, and answer them from chair two. Be challenging with yourself!

- This sounds like a serious issue for you. Are you willing to put some effort into solving this?

- What are the facts surrounding this issue? (Don't be fobbed off with impressions, or generalities.)

- What is the real impact of this on you and on others?

- What will happen if you don't solve this issue?

- How exactly would you like things to be when this is solved?

- What are you willing to do, or lose or say goodbye to so that this can happen?

- So what are you going to commit to?

- Can I have that in writing?

Quick wins

- Get into an argument, but don't lose your temper.

- Find something in your neighbourhood that you care about and make a fuss.

- Invite other people to talk openly about their discomforts.

- Describe your emotions about an issue to someone you wouldn't normally say this to.

- Commit openly to resolving an irritating issue and pursue it doggedly with the help of others.

- Complain about something that you have bought. Take it back to the shop. Be specific and say exactly what you want instead of this.

- Ask someone who isn't getting around to something what's stopping them from doing it.

- Ask a colleague what they are hoping you won't ask them.

- Don't talk about people, talk to them (this is challenging!).

- Extract trivial and insensitive remarks when you are talking to people who matter to you.

- When someone else whines about a colleague, ask them when they are going to confront that person about their behaviour, and if not, why not.

- Name a problem that no one else is brave enough to name.

- Speak only of things that seem to matter; speak only from the heart.

- Apologize to people to whom you have behaved badly.

- Praise people whom you meant to praise months ago, and apologize for not getting around to it. Commit to doing better next time.

- Use silence when emotion runs high. This will slow down the conversation and give everyone time to say what they really think or feel.

Playful exercises

In a safe environment, try exaggerating the Edgy Catalyser role. Make an enormous fuss about a problem you would like to see solved, or be a massive thorn in someone's side. See how long you can keep it up.

Imagine a situation in which it would be extremely difficult to be an Edgy Catalyser, eg a patient at the dentist, a motorist who has just been pulled up for a traffic offence, an inanimate object such as a mobile phone, a vicar at a funeral. Get a group together and try out being an Edgy Catalyser in each of these situations.

DEVELOPING THE VISIONARY MOTIVATOR IN YOU

Rate yourself as a Visionary Motivator

Score yourself from 1 to 5 (1 = strongly disagree, 2 = disagree, 3 = agree a little, 4 = agree, 5 strongly agree):

1. I'm able to set out a vision and articulate its component parts meaningfully to others.

2. I demonstrate the confidence to bring people along with me.

3. I genuinely believe that given the will, people can achieve anything.

4. I'm skilled at turning problems into solutions.

5. I'm emotionally resilient and bounce back easily and quickly.

6. I enjoy getting people on board with my ideas.

7. I see coaching as a real force in motivating people.

8. I truly believe that you have to win the hearts and minds of people in any change situation.

9. I think positive and see the glass as half full rather than half empty.

10. I can hold the vision long enough and strong enough for people to step into it.

Check these scores with your colleagues – especially the people you manage.

Score analysis

If you score more than 30 then you are well on the way to mastering the Visionary Motivator role. If you score less than 25, try practising the role using the exercises listed below. If you score less than 20, you may have to concede defeat and ensure that you include a Visionary Motivator on your leadership team.

Practising the role

Exercise 1

Affirmations

An affirmation is a positive statement describing the way that you want to be. It is important that the statement is:

- Personal – 'I am always enthusiastic when it comes to work!' It is you that this is about and it's as specific as you can make it.

- Present tense – '**I am always** enthusiastic when it comes to work!' It is not in the future, it's right now.

- Positive – 'I am always **enthusiastic** when it comes to work!' Describing a positive attribute, not the absence of a negative attribute.

- Potent – 'I am always **enthusiastic** when it comes to **work**!' Using words that mean something to you.

Try writing your own affirmation. Put it on a card and read it out 10 times a day. As you do so, remember to imagine what you would feel, what you would see, what you would hear if it were true.

Visualizations

Visualizations are very similar to affirmations but focus on a positive, present mental image. Effective visualizations require you to enter a relaxed state where you imagine a specific example of the way you want to be. You imagine what you and others would see, what would be heard and what would be felt. Using all your senses you imagine yourself achieving the specific goal. You need to practise this regularly.

Once you get a good sense of your own imagined future, you can try bringing some of those thoughts and feelings into your life even sooner. For instance, if you visualize going for long walks with your partner when you have more time, try making time now. Go for a walk tomorrow. This illustrates the power of visualizing the future; it can give us energy for now.

Exercise 2

Buy or borrow a copy of Edward De Bono's *Six Thinking Hats*. Read up on the Yellow Hat and try it out for size. In De Bono's words: 'Yellow Hat: This hat finds reasons why something will work and why it will offer benefits. It can be used in looking forward to the results of some proposed action. It can also be used to find something of value in what has already happened.'

Take a tricky situation you are currently familiar with – personal, organizational or global – and think of all the positive outcomes that are possible. Write them down and then try to double the number of positive outcomes in your list. Your next task is to convince a friend or colleague that these outcomes can really be achieved. Then try to convince the most cynical colleague you can find.

Exercise 3

This is an opportunity for you to experiment with your leadership voice and to receive the type of feedback you don't normally get.

Choose a couple of close friends or work colleagues to 'practise' on.

Spend ten minutes preparing a two-minute talk that is so powerful and persuasive that your audience cannot fail to follow you. Make the topic a real initiative that you would like to progress at work or in your private life or community. Think of a real audience that you want to address (no matter how big or small). You'll need to brief your chosen audience what role(s) to take, eg operations manager, CFO, technician etc.

You should then do your two-minute presentation as if you're on TV (ie no interaction at all).

Then sit down and get the audience to discuss your talk as if you're not there, and as if they were still in role.

Then take a deep breath (no discussion) and try again.

Exercise 4

Reframing

Reframing is a technique for reducing feelings and thoughts that impact negatively on performance. Do you get daunted going in to see the senior management team? Currently you see them looming large, full of colour, vitality and menacing presence?

Imagine them in the boardroom, but this time visualize them all in grey. Maybe shrink them in size as you would a piece of clip art in a document that you are word-processing. Turn down their volume so they sound quite quiet. Run through this several times and see what effect it has on your anxiety.

Quick wins

- Try doing a job in an unusual way. It may not work, but you will learn something.

- Think of something important to you now. Imagine what might happen with this in the future. Try to think of a number of different scenarios.

- If you have a 'hunch', take some notice of it and follow it up.

- Make an effort to think about something in a conceptual or abstract manner. Use descriptive or unusual words, or draw a picture to represent it.

- Run a brainstorming session; help people to build on their ideas.

- Ask a couple of people to give you some feedback on your latest plan for work/hobby/holiday; be enthusiastic when you describe it.

- Talk about whatever you are passionate about – anything from yoga to yachting. Use colourful language. Don't worry if people switch off. Instead, notice what switches them on.

- Try to describe your job or role in life in an unusual way. For instance, a management consultant might call himself an 'organizational midwife; present at the birth of all the best projects'. A bricklayer might describe his job as 'building to house the human spirit'. Then use this to introduce yourself and notice what happens.

- Take a risk and share your ideas for the future at your next team meeting. Take feedback.

- Keep in touch with what is going on in the outside world and try to use other people's ideas to inform your own.

- Think about the worst possible change that might happen to you and your team at work. Now list all the possible advantages of that change, and make some notes on how you would persuade the team that this is a good idea.

- Offer to lead on the next change initiative.

- If you normally include a lot of detail in your arguments, try leaving that out completely.

- Observe how others bring energy to group sessions. What can you learn from them?

- Think about a group of colleagues or friends or your family. If you wanted to persuade them of a particular course of action, think about what aspect of that idea would appeal to each person.

- Make an effort to praise someone when they do something right – be it a co-worker, a shop assistant, a friend or enemy!

Playful exercises

In a safe environment, try exaggerating the Visionary Motivator role. Make an impassioned speech about the future of your wardrobe, or your monthly report, or your family pet, or something that you find essentially mundane.

Imagine a situation in which it would be a big challenge for you to be a Visionary Motivator. For example, present your vision for converting the local fish and chip shop into…, address a group of lemmings about the future, talk to your neighbour about the possibility of going on holiday together…

DEVELOPING THE MEASURED CONNECTOR IN YOU

Rate yourself as a Measured Connector

Score yourself from 1 to 5 (1 = strongly disagree, 2 = disagree, 3 = agree a little, 4 = agree, 5 strongly agree):

1. ° I am interested in other people's agendas and am able to tune into them.

2. I am seen as a person of high integrity whom people can trust.

3. I enjoy letting other people shine.

4. I am able to keep calm and remain supportive and clear when others are losing their cool.

5. I have a high level of drive to achieve medium- to long-range organizational goals, and don't get diverted by others' or my own self-importance.

6. I am patient when others are struggling to come up with an idea or a solution.

7. I habitually put different people together to discuss important challenges.

8. I have a well-developed sense of purpose that guides everything that I do.

9. I encourage people to experiment and try things out.

10. I have an ability to be clear in complex situations, without over-simplifying things.

Check these scores with your colleagues – especially the people you manage.

Score analysis

If you score more than 30 then you are well on the way to mastering the Measured Connector role. If you score less than 25, try practising the role using the exercises listed below. If you score less than 20, you may have to concede defeat and ensure that you include a Measured Connector on your leadership team.

Practising the role

Exercise 1

Create a role play involving two other people which is set in your own sitting room. Imagine a situation of conflict and mayhem as the family prepares for your wedding. Your job is to stay calm and help the two other family members to remember the purpose of the day, and try to help them to tune into each other's agendas and find common needs. Perhaps one person could play your anxious mother who doesn't get on with your partner's parents. The other could play one of your siblings who wants to get the whole thing over with so he/she can watch Wimbledon on TV.

Review how you did, how difficult or easy you found it to be calm and connecting, and the effect that your behaviour had on each of the 'family members'.

Exercise 2

Think of something you would like to change within your local community. Perhaps you would like to see weekly recycling collections, or an improvement in the local park facilities. Try to encapsulate the purpose of the change in a couple of short crisp sentences, and identify three principles you would like to stick to as you go about making this happen. Make a list of all the people who would be important stakeholders were you to embark on this initiative and think about how to engage each stakeholder by considering what their separate agendas are and what connects them to each other. If you don't know, try asking around. You might learn something! Who would you get together first?

Exercise 3

Focus on a work-based situation and identify two individuals whom you think need to be talking to each other to further the effectiveness of the organization in some way. Rehearse different ways of encouraging them to get together. Try some sensible approaches, remembering to be clear about what you think they each might gain from the conversation, and how it might be a good idea for the organization as a whole. Try exaggerating your approach either by being very subtle and obscure, or by using a ridiculously hard sell.

Once you have experimented in the privacy of your own bedroom, in the mirror maybe, try it out in reality.

Quick wins

- Employ tact at all times; preserve other people's dignity even when they are being unreasonable.

- If you sense a conflict brewing, try to raise it to the surface and help people to confront the issue in a contained way. Provide some ground-rules to help them to have a sensible conversation.

- Always ask people what's important to them – begin to make a habit of this, especially in organizational life.

- Keep a record of people's names, contact details and interests.

- Initiate discussions with other groups to see whether you can help them.

- Think beyond the personal relationships in your organization and think about how things work systemically. This means about what would happen in organizational life even if different people were in the roles (eg culturally influenced activities such as senior management leaving junior managers waiting for hours before they present to the senior management team meeting).

- Pick three people in your organization with whom you wouldn't normally have contact... find out what they do and how that helps the organization meet its purpose.

- Work on enabling people to trust you by revealing things about yourself – your family, hobbies, what you care about, what worries you.

- If you normally over-structure meetings, try letting others speak first and practise building on their ideas instead of initiating everything.

- If you normally over-structure meetings, try negotiating the outcomes and process right at the start, and let the meeting run itself. Chip in to remind people of the purpose if you need to.

● Get good at recognizing your own emotional state by paying attention to the physical signs that you experience in situations where you are nervous, anxious, excited, guilty, ashamed or angry.

● Start doing yoga or meditation (or long walks) to get good at shielding yourself from intrusive thoughts.

● Consciously try to become a role model of your own principles, eg always admit when you have got something wrong, and always receive criticism graciously.

● Practise being present. This means giving the current situation your undivided attention – switch your phone off, listen well, ensure that you can see everyone.

● Know your 'hot buttons' (ie know what behaviours in other people trigger your anger or anxiety), and even when they are pressed, invite yourself to stay steady and resilient. Allow others to use your containing calm as a way of providing a safe, structured place to air a difficult issue.

● Develop a set of crisp ground-rules to govern a complex change process, or organizational setting. Try to stick to these, giving feedback when they are transgressed.

Playful exercises

In a safe environment, try exaggerating the Measured Connector role. Try bringing together people who really aren't connected at all, eg introduce your company's stationery suppliers to a prospective client of the company, or introduce the technical people designing the customer database to the company counsellor. Experiment with different ways in which you would try to get them to see how much they have in common.

Try doing what a Measured Connector would never do. With a few friends, create an imaginary company networking event and experiment with some really crass and disrespectful introductions between people.

DEVELOPING THE TENACIOUS IMPLEMENTER IN YOU

Rate yourself as a Tenacious Implementer

Score yourself from 1 to 5 (1 = strongly disagree, 2 = disagree, 3 = agree a little, 4 = agree, 5 strongly agree):

1.   I am deeply interested in the task and how it gets done.

2.   I expect people to do what they say they are going to do, and if they don't I start to become quite irritated (although I don't always show it).

3.   I don't like going back on a decision, although I will do it when necessary.

4.   People say that I win them over or wear them down with my persistence.

5.   I have a lot of energy for the job and tend to be called in when there is a mess to sort out.

6.   I am good at understanding and remembering technical and managerial details.

7.   I can take a large, long-range project and easily break it down into manageable chunks – project management comes naturally to me.

8.   I worry about the near future more than I worry about the long-range future.

9.   I can interface well with stakeholders (but I don't necessarily enjoy that part of the job).

10. I am good at eliciting clear requirements from people, and then keeping to the brief.

Check these scores with your colleagues – especially the people you manage.

Score analysis

If you score more than 30 then you are well on the way to mastering the Tenacious Implementer role. If you score less than 25, try practising the role using the exercises listed below. If you score less than 20, you may have to concede defeat and ensure that you include a Tenacious Implementer on your leadership team.

Practising the role

Exercise 1

Identify something practical that you want to achieve at home, such as a decorating or renovation project, or changing something in your garden. Plan out absolutely all the activities you will need to carry out to achieve your goal, and try to estimate how long it will all take. Don't use gut feel; instead, break things down and estimate the effort separately.

Share your plan with a friend and commit to doing it. Talk through what might possibly go wrong to divert you from achieving this goal in the agreed timescale, such as bad weather, or something more interesting turning up. Then make sure you plan in some contingency, or do something that lessens the likelihood of these obstacles getting in your way.

Exercise 2

Run a role play with a friend in which you wish to persuade her to do something that she doesn't want to do, like get her hair cut or buy a new car. Don't stop until you have tried all the different arguments for doing it that you can think of. Think very broadly and widely and don't worry about being 'sensible' – you're trying to find a solution which just might work. Try asking the individual what's getting in the way, and then work on persuading him or her that this obstacle isn't a problem at all. See how long it takes to wear the other person down.

Exercise 3

Select a project at work that you would like to approach in a more rigorous way. Choose something that is very task-focused, technical in nature or well defined. An IT system update or the introduction of a new process would be a good choice.

Plan this project out in detail, and chunk it into stages with milestones, giving each milestone a fixed date. Identify all the different stakeholders that you need to keep on board, and list the people within your own unit whose help you need. Plan a series of short meetings with all these people, each with a fairly tight agenda to get everyone engaged and on board. Make sure they all have a copy of the plan, and organize regular updates for you and all the immediate team.

Use this method to carry out the project. Have a conversation with your boss about how it went.

Quick wins

- Complete a task you have been meaning to do for a long time and reward yourself well.

- Make a plan to challenge something complex. Stick it up on the wall and stick a moveable arrow on it showing progress.

- Be on time for every meeting for the next week.

- Use facts to argue a point instead of feelings.

- Next time someone disagrees with you, stick with your initial point a bit longer.

- Give up joking around for the next three days. Take things more seriously.

- Use simple, uncomplicated language in your next e-mail.

- In your next PowerPoint presentation, or your next report, use some graphs or statistics to back up your point.

- Next time you initiate a piece of work, agree standards with your team before you begin, and stick to them.

- Set goals every day, and review how you did at the end of the day. A week later, stretch the goal.

- Find out exactly what someone in your organization needs, write it down, and deliver it to them on an agreed date.

- Try to improve your eye for detail by noticing small things on your journey to work, the price of things at the supermarket, listening to the actual words people say and writing them down.

- Notice how reliable you are. Do you do what you say you will do? Try to improve this.

- Next time you meet with a friend, ask about the progress of a task or project they are involved in, rather than asking about how they are.

- Think of a situation at work or at home in which you are deeply involved and try to write a completely objective description of what has happened so far, who is involved, and what everyone wants and needs.

- Be firmer about performance levels and goals.

- Say no to unproductive activities, and prune your network, extracting those to whom you are unquestionably loyal even though it doesn't do you or your project any good.

Playful exercises

In a safe environment, try exaggerating the Tenacious Implementer role. Imagine you are organizing a birthday party for a three-year-old. Become like a bulldozer for the plan, ignoring all objections, and being blind to all sensitivities.

Imagine a situation in which it would be a big challenge for you to be a Tenacious Implementer, eg planning the rest of your life, or planning your dog's week. With a few friends, try playing out this scenario and see what spontaneously emerges.

DEVELOPING THE THOUGHTFUL ARCHITECT IN YOU

Rate yourself as a Thoughtful Architect

Score yourself from 1 to 5 (1 = strongly disagree, 2 = disagree, 3 = agree a little, 4 = agree, 5 strongly agree):

1. I will always take time out to think things through.
2. I am good at seeing the big picture and how the different parts of a complex problem fit together.
3. I think a lot about the future and can spot where elements of the vision don't stack up.
4. I will not be hurried into making reactive decisions.
5. I can stand my ground and argue my case thoughtfully, broadly and deeply and from a number of different perspectives.
6. I won't compromise the strategy for the sake of short-term tactics.
7. I spend time scanning the environment and understand what's on the horizon.
8. I make sense of the internal organization and see what needs to be changed to fit with future challenges.
9. I am always open to new ideas about the future as long as they make sense.
10. I believe conceptual models of the world have a use in developing strategy.

Check these scores with your colleagues – especially the people you manage.

Score analysis

If you score more than 30 then you are well on the way to mastering the Thoughtful Architect role. If you score less than 25, try practising the role using the exercises listed below. If you score less than 20, you may have to concede defeat and ensure that you include a Thoughtful Architect on your leadership team.

Practising the role

Exercise 1

Imagine you have to explore a certain part of your local geography – perhaps some hills or mountain range in the locality. Get a large-scale walking map and begin to spot some interesting features which you might like to visit. Plan some alternative routes to and from these places, taking into account the terrain and the connections between the different places. You might also like to see the terrain from a number of different perspectives – for example, different-scale maps reveal different features, a road map will be different from one showing fauna and flora, or one showing ancient Roman remains. A bus map or a population density map would also show the terrain from different perspectives. A weather or climate map illustrates yet another perspective.

Reflect upon how you might start to see your organization and the environment that it's in from different perspectives. What are the interesting features in your organization? What are the different systems within the organization and how permeable is the organization to outside influences?

Exercise 2

Buy a strategy book or borrow one from a friend – it doesn't have to be complex – but it should contain a few of the strategic analysis planning models in common use. Look on the internet for references to PEST or PESTLE analysis and McKinsey's 7Ss and undertake a brief strategic review of your organization or your department – perhaps even you and your family!

Develop a SWOT analysis and build some strategies to exploit the strengths and opportunities and to mitigate the weaknesses and threats.

Look at where you are in the organization and – with your new knowledge – decide what needs to be changed, develop a plan and start talking to people about it. Start by asking other people how they see the world shaping up – collate two or three people's views to feed into your own.

Exercise 3

As you scan the environment and scrutinize your particular operating environment for what might happen in the future, you'll
recognize some things that you're pretty sure will happen while other
things might have some chance of happening. And with some they
may or may not happen – you just don't know the probability. Each
will have different meanings when viewed within the overall context
of the future.

Rather than take a view on just one set of circumstances happening
and planning for that, construct a number of different future
scenarios and see how well placed the organization is to meet and
master each of those.

Some managers will simply construct a best-case scenario and a
worst-case scenario and then plumb for something in between.
However, the purpose of developing the scenarios is to tease out and
test organizational capabilities and capacity to meet these scenarios
and to develop local strategies that will be able to exploit some of the
opportunities and mitigate some of the threats.

Exercise 4

Get hold of a copy of _Making Sense of Change Management_ (Cameron
and Green, 2004) where you'll find a number of different perspectives on change. Look at change from an individual, team and organizational perspective. The book offers a range of models and lenses
through which you can conceptualize strategic change. It also has a
chapter on the different roles leaders play in change. Its underlying
philosophy is that there is no one right way to manage or lead
change and you, as Thoughtful Architect, need to think the situation
through and reach your own conclusion.

Quick wins

- Try to keep an open mind about those around you rather than
  making hasty judgements.

- Seek out some technical/expert books and journals that cover your
  current work area. Read these and inwardly digest.

- Work with someone who is an accomplished strategist to devise lots of different ways of seeing the future for your organization, community or neighbourhood.

- Look at trends and predictions for your industry; find these on the internet.

- Find out who is doing great things in your line of work. Try to meet the people involved, or look them up on the internet and read about their latest activities.

- Devote more time to considering things more deeply and with more concentration.

- Take time to be on your own and listen to yourself, understanding that you have an inner life.

- Build up your one-to-one relationships so that you experience these at greater depth.

- Ask questions of others and listen carefully to the answers. Make notes and try to pull all the ideas together into a bigger picture.

- Think carefully before acting and then act.

- Think of the way a process at work is designed, or the way a department is structured. Completely redesign that process or structure in two different ways and compare the three designs using a set of success criteria.

- Make an effort to think about something in a conceptual or abstract manner.

- See if you can think ahead and plan something creative for the future.

- Find out about the history of your organization or department. How have things changed in the last 10 years, and what prompted these shifts?

- Set some key principles that underpin the work of your division or unit.

- Loosen the structure you have in meetings, or the format that is used to write reports.

- Offer yourself as an objective, dispassionate sounding board for someone else's ideas.

- Come up with five sentences that summarize what is important to you in life.

- Refuse to get bogged down in details.

- Only contribute to discussions if you feel it is really worthwhile.

Playful exercises

In a safe environment, try exaggerating the Thoughtful Architect role. For example, interview someone for a straightforward role in the company, and ask them all sorts of semi-relevant high-level conceptual questions, or critique a document about cleaning the communal microwave in the light of its possible links with the organization's five-year strategy.

Do what a Thoughtful Architect would never do; dumb down the company strategy.

14

The shadow side

When you step into a leadership role, your relationships with people begin to change. You might make a lot of friends, or you might start to lose all your friends. People treat you differently, not because of who you are but because of the role you're playing. People see you in a different light. They might also begin to project their hopes and fears onto you. They begin to study you for any hint of ulterior motive, they try to work out what you really think, and they start to attempt to predict what you might actually do.

At the same time something happens inside you. In the worst case this might lead to you becoming corrupted by the power of your leadership position. Vaclav Havel, former Czech president, wrote an interesting piece on the corrupting influence of power, which illustrates how easy it is to move from a simple act that any leader might do, to abusing power completely. Havel was pressured for time, but had a dentist's appointment to attend. He considered whether or not he should use a state vehicle to go to the dentist, which would save him time and allow him to concentrate on important matters of state. Then he started to wonder whether the disruption to the Prague traffic as his motorcade swept through the city was too high a cost for others to pay. Then he started to become concerned that if he used his position to secure advantage for such a trivial matter, this might become the thin end of the wedge for ever greater abuses of power.

In this chapter we look at some of the shadowy aspects of power and leadership, of which leaders and followers need to be aware. We identify what this 'shadow side of leadership' is, what its effects might be, explore the shadow side of each of the five leadership roles, and suggest some strategies which can be used to mitigate the potential excesses of the shadow side.

LEADERS ON A BAD DAY

If we look at a typical list of leadership traits, the shadow side of leadership can be seen as the dysfunctional or extreme version of an initially very effective way of doing things. Table 14.1 illustrates this.

Table 14.1   Effective leadership traits and their associated dysfunctions

Effective traits	Dysfunctional traits
Adaptable to situations	Unreliable
Alert to situations	Paranoid
Ambitious and achievement-oriented	Self-obsessed
Assertive	Pushy
Cooperative	Pushover
Decisive	Knee-jerk reactor, rigid
Dependable	Fixed
Dominant	Bullying
Energetic	Manic
Persistent	Pig-headed
Self-confident	Arrogant
Tolerant of stress	Aloof

KNOWING YOUR OWN SHADOW

When we enter a situation, we tend to bring with us our baggage from our past. Our formative years have a critical effect on who we are, how we present to the world and how we react to situations. Our earlier relationships with significant figures (mother, father, siblings) can cause us to repeat patterns that might have been useful then but are very often inappropriate now. For example, this might mean extreme reactions such as dissociation or anger. This can lead to seemingly irrational behaviour in a current, adult situation.

In addition to this, each of us has an innate personality that means we respond to different types of communication in different ways, sometimes becoming energized, but sometimes becoming stressed and anxious. These things can happen below the level of awareness and can be a great source of confluence or conflict with people of a different type. Again, we can end up behaving in ways which don't match our intent.

Our life experiences can also lead us to misjudge people and situations, using the scars from old wounds to help us to tackle completely different circumstances. In this way we behave in an inappropriate or unhelpful way, with the resulting unintended reactions from others.

So the key to understanding and mastering your shadow is to surface it in all its manifestations: by discovering where your blind spots are; what your triggers are; checking out how you interact with others and noticing where you typically come into conflict with them.

LEADERS AND THE SHADOW

Napoleon once said that 'leaders are dealers in hope'. This is often played out by followers who want the leader to be their knight in shining armour who can resolve any situation. People may imagine the leader to be the messiah who is not only all-knowing, but is capable of taking them to the promised land. Of course this is an impossible position to be put in for leaders and followers alike, rather like the 'honeymoon period' which new partnerships experience. Eventually people will realize that the leader has flaws, that they are only human after all, and that everyone is at least partly responsible for how things turn out. However, the deflation this brings can have a tremendously demotivating effect.

When followers have unrealistic expectations of leaders, a number of things begin to happen:

- Leaders begin to believe that they really do know everything and that they are infallible in the decisions they make.

- Leaders surround themselves with people whom they trust and who are in agreement with them.

- Leaders lose touch with reality by being told only the things that they want to hear, and don't connect into the life and soul of the organization.

- Leaders become unsure of whom to trust and then feel isolated.

- Followers become overly subservient and deferential (like the lowest of the low) or alternatively antagonistic and rebellious (like the child or adolescent). Neither stance aids effective organizational working.

Leaders can also become the emotional guide for the followers and can feel this as quite a heavy burden, often feeling the need to be optimistic and positive; always needing to show confidence; always being 'on duty'. All this can add further to a leaders' challenge to remain self-aware and balanced, ensuring that the shadow side is kept in the background, rather than getting the upper hand.

THE SHADOW SIDE OF THE FIVE LEADERSHIP ROLES

Edgy Catalyser

Being an Edgy Catalyser is a subtle business. Too much can switch people off; too little goes unnoticed. On a bad day, the Edgy Catalyser can take the habit of pointing things out to extremes, being more concerned with highlighting what is wrong than engaging people in the need to do things differently. This can then have the effect of turning people off and increasing resistance.

Edgy Catalysers can also become dysfunctional when they focus too much on what's going wrong and how to change it, and too little on what's going right and how to support it.

If Edgy Catalysers let their drive to achieve run riot, they then appear overly driven to achieve the ultimate goals of performance improvement and completely ignore the sensitivities of the people involved. On a bad day this may result in behaviour such as obstinacy, crassness and bullying.

They can sometimes become rather obsessive about pace. Their habit of making a drama out of a crisis may lead to them becoming more and more energized to bulldoze their way through things rather than loosening up and taking things at a more natural pace. Typically they may become more aggressive, more insistent, more persistent in letting people know what's right and wrong, rather than engaging people in the process of change. They become more coercive and corrosive, when it would be better to be less so. Taken to extremes, they can come to believe that they are always right; they can adopt an uncompromising attitude and believe that others 'need to understand' something about the situation rather than they themselves having something to learn.

In summary, the Edgy Catalyser in shadow mode can be overly critical and may disengage people; can appear more interested in breaking things than building things; might be seen to be random and a loose cannon rather than planned and controlled; and can be interfering, impatient and unwilling to think things through. Edgy Catalysers need to be able to strike the right balance between fulfilling their role and understanding the immediate and longer-term implications and impact that they have on the individuals and groups they interact with.

Visionary Motivator

The Visionary Motivator operates from a fundamental belief in the benefits of the future vision for all those involved. However, this can become more of a missionary zeal than a vision, which may overwhelm normal people who might like to go along at their own pace, treating the vision as something that's way off in the distance, maybe slightly out of reach and intangible. This reaction to the Visionary Motivator's passionate talk might just make things worse. 'Normal' people can be seen as sceptics or cynics and therefore ideal material for conversion to the true faith!

Visionary Motivators have such high energy and enthusiasm that they can come across as fake, or even worse, slightly unhinged. This can turn more people off than on. They sometimes appear superhuman, bouncing back from any setback, becoming totally unstoppable and potentially becoming someone to either make fun of or hide from.

Seeing the world through rose-tinted glasses can give followers a great lift. The downside of the over-positive Visionary Motivator is that he or she demands high levels of positivity from everyone else too. The effect of this atmosphere of relentlessly upbeat pronouncements can be very damaging to productivity and to morale. The idea that you are either 'on the bus or off it' divides the world into two camps and doesn't allow for nuances. Being pessimistic or angry or depressed can sometimes be useful and even transformational. Visionary Motivators can often not accept that people need to make sense of changes – and feel a huge range of emotions during the process of change – in their own ways and at their own paces.

The Visionary Motivator can appear at times to be someone who has been brainwashed into accepting and embracing the vision without a moment's thought and is also trying to brainwash everyone else down the same route.

In summary, the Visionary Motivator in shadow mode can be seen to accentuate the positive too much and be reluctant to hear the negatives or even to be realistic about problems. The extreme Visionary Motivator might leave people behind, or become a figure of fun through excessive bounce-back-ability, or turn into an over-the-top evangelist that others avoid. Visionary Motivators have to strike the right balance between maintaining their positive outlook on life and recognizing that other people won't necessarily share their enthusiasm wholeheartedly all the time.

Measured Connector

The shadow side of the Measured Connector can take a while to emerge. They tend to be calmer and more evenly paced in their habits than the Edgy Catalyser and Visionary Motivator, so their idiosyncrasies are less immediately visible.

Measured Connectors are so focused on the big and broad task of connecting individuals around a bigger sense of purpose that they may become fuzzy or erratic, neglecting the details of day-to-day and month-to-month performance. Their focus on goals may not be concrete enough for some, and in extreme situations, the Measured Connector's lack of attention to specific targets can be seen as irresponsible.

Measured Connectors see patterns everywhere, and may start to believe that everything in organizational life is redolent with meaning. They might over-analyse situations to extract their symbolism or to uncover hidden agendas where there sometimes are none.

On a bad day, Measured Connectors want to believe that every organizational activity must be explicitly connected and that even the most uninvolved and distant stakeholders need to be catered for and included. They might lack the focus and pragmatism that's needed to make their way through a complex situation, ignoring some stakeholders and leaving out some minor but important issues.

Measured Connectors tend to be both appreciative of people's contributions and affirming and respectful of their different agendas. In the extreme, this tendency can be seen as not wanting to upset the applecart or not being willing to ruffle people's feathers. They might fail to take a stand on an issue or say what needs to be said, because they fear diminishing the role of others.

In summary, the Measured Connector in shadow mode can lack focus on the day-to-day goals and performance indicators and has a tendency to overemphasize the need for everyone to be involved. In extreme situations, the Measured Connector sees meaning and connection where perhaps none exists and may lack the personal energy and passion required to make a stand about what needs to be done or what the ground-rules are. The Measured Connector needs to ensure a balance between paying attention to the connectivity of the organization and the need for ongoing delivery and concrete thinking.

Tenacious Implementer

The Tenacious Implementer has the propensity to be highly persistent in the pursuit of project goals. In extremis, this can translate into blinkered behaviour such as taking a fixed view of what needs to be achieved, and ignoring all other views.

In shadow mode, Tenacious Implementers acquire tunnel vision. They begin to exclude other possibilities and attempt to railroad their plan through, come what may. Obstacles in their way, including other people's agendas, perceptions and sensitivities, are bulldozed away. Once the project plan has been agreed, the Tenacious Implementer can see it as their role and their obligation to deliver on the plan, at whatever cost to others. Even when under extreme pressure to shift timescales owing to unexpected problems, they may refuse to entertain the need for any readjustment, which may lead to more stress and more delivery problems.

If you want to hurry a Tenacious Implementer, you may need to gird your loins! In shadow mode they can become exceptionally stubborn, saying the equivalent of 'the plan is the plan and I'm not changing it for anyone'. If outside factors change, such as a customer's product launch date, the extreme Tenacious Implementer may need a lot of persuading to re-plan the project and find a way of delivering a bit earlier.

Tenacious Implementers don't like the idea of keeping their options open or allowing things to emerge as the change progresses. Being structured, systematized and scheduled are their most effective traits. However, these qualities, taken to extremes, can become part of the cause of project failure. Tenacious Implementers may not stop to look at the bigger picture to see where things or people need to be better joined up. They may fail to see that the project is inextricably connected to the way change is developing within the organization and that the project in isolation is just one part of the jigsaw. The jigsaw itself needs to be recognized by the Tenacious Implementer and he or she needs to develop an understanding of how the pieces fit together.

In summary, the Tenacious Implementer in shadow mode may appear to be railroading other people towards an unworkable solution or timescale without adapting to changing circumstances. They can also lose sight of the organizational objectives, and become too focused on delivering their piece of the jigsaw. The Tenacious Implementer will need to practise the art of remaining true to their own sense of focus and ability to deliver, while holding the possibility that requirements might shift, the organizational context may change and that people and technology don't act in totally predictable ways.

Thoughtful Architect

The Thoughtful Architect needs the time and space to think things through to be able to come up with his or her grand designs. However, the shadow side of this role can emerge when there's a pressurized environment and there just isn't the time or the space available.

Paralysis by analysis can take root in the Thoughtful Architect, or sometimes a manifestation of what we call 'multiple choice neurosis'. The latter occurs when Thoughtful Architects just can't make a decision because they are faced with a number of conflicting choices which they themselves generated!

The other aspect of the Thoughtful Architect's shadow which can cause a great deal of frustration in others is the need for every plan or any decision to fit neatly into the bigger picture. Most managers accept compromise and work with the art of the possible. However, the Thoughtful Architect from their lofty and strategic tower can some-times fail to see the pragmatic need to get something working opera-tionally now, rather than getting the perfect design.

When you couple helicopter thinking with the desire to work things out on their own or with like-minded people, you can begin to see how Thoughtful Architects on a bad day might appear to be quite arrogant. Having thought through all the possibilities, they descend triumphantly from the mountain with their grand strategy and are sometimes taken aback when people dare to disagree or criticize. Strangely, it is they themselves who can come across as the principal critics of anyone else's ideas or proposals.

In summary, the Thoughtful Architect in shadow mode can become paralysed by possibilities or obsessed by making everything fit together conceptually. They might also appear arrogant or over-critical of other people's ideas. The Thoughtful Architect needs to balance their ability to come up with conceptually watertight strategies with the need to meet others in their domain rather than always doing things on their own terms. Practising making decisions and enacting strategies when not fully complete is one way to begin.

SURFACING THE SHADOW

Many psychologists have written extensively on the shadow side of life (notably Carl Jung, see Zweig and Abrams (1990)). They do not say that the shadow is a bad thing which should be eradicated. The shadow is a normal and natural side of humanity, often repressed or labelled as 'bad', which is what makes it so hard to recognize in ourselves. The challenge is how to be aware of the shadow and then how to deal with it, because if you fail to do this, all sorts of dysfunctions start to appear in others around you.

One of the tasks of leadership is to be aware of the shadow and be able to work with it constructively. Key aspects are to:

- Understand what the shadow is.

- See why the shadow matters in organizations and in times of change.

- Develop ways of spotting it within oneself, within others and the organization at large.

- Increase knowledge and understanding to be able to make sense of shadow dynamics.

- Improve one's skills in managing the shadow.

SOME PRACTICAL IDEAS FOR WORKING WITH THE SHADOW

Egan (1994) discusses the shadow in organizations in great depth and suggests a number of practical things you can do to surface the shadow and deal with it. He suggests you need to focus your attention on the shadow side during times of change, in addition to all the other things you are doing:

- Legitimize the search for and naming of blind spots.

- Ask the questions behind the questions.

- Welcome new perspectives from others.

- Think about ways you might be in the dark.

- Sit up when you are surprised by behaviour or events.

- Identify the consequences of not discussing the issue.

- Use a confidant to discuss fears about negative consequences.

- Identify issues that you're reluctant to discuss.

- Identify issues that others are reluctant to discuss.

- Develop the ability to name the issue, having put yourself in the recipient's shoes first.

- Turn embarrassment into learning.

- Monitor self-interest.

- Use shared problem-solving methodology.

In Table 14.2, Heifetz (1994) addresses what leaders need to do to maintain their sanity and equilibrium whilst undertaking their leadership roles. He advises leaders to depersonalize criticism of themselves, stay strategic to avoid getting personal, find a critical friend to talk to, know themselves well, guard reflection time carefully and keep focused on a clear sense of purpose.

Table 14.2 Adapted from Heifetz (1994) in *Leadership Without Easy Answers*

Distinguish self from role	Be sure to understand that you are not your role. People will respond to your role with a variety of emotions and behaviours. In times of change these can be quite powerful and sometimes irrational. Do not take these personally.
Externalize the conflict	By distinguishing self from role you can externalize any conflict, focusing attention on the issues not the personalities. You can redirect attention back to the challenge, staying strategic and emphasizing where you want to get to, what you want to achieve.
Use partners	Every person who leads will, from time to time, need support and challenge in distinguishing self from role and keeping the issues impersonal. Find and use people whom you can trust both as a confidant (to offload emotionally) and as a critical friend (to test your thinking). Establishing who you have in your network that can fulfil this role is important.

Listen, using oneself as data	Self-knowledge is key to being able to understand how you might distort incoming communications and how you might interpret data and make decisions based on your personality preferences. Reflecting on daily actions, living with a certain degree of doubt about whether we are making all the right decisions, behaving in the most appropriate ways, using others to feed back the consequences of our actions and any blind spots are all ways we can develop our self-knowledge.
Find a sanctuary	Leaders are busy people with multiple demands being placed upon them by others as well as themselves. Leaders need time and space to reflect upon the direction, the challenges, the actions. Either with trusted others or with themselves they need to build into their busy schedules space where they can fulfil the inner tasks of leadership.
Preserve a sense of purpose	'Leadership requires a sense of purpose – the capacity to find the values that make risk-taking meaningful.' Returning on a regular basis to the question 'what is our purpose?', holding it dear, assists in times of discomfort and, along with the necessary reflection on the course of action and consequences of that action, creates a golden thread running through the leadership of change.

In conclusion, the shadow side of leadership can be a powerful force which, if left unchecked, will undermine a leader's ability to act well in the various roles he or she needs to fill in order to serve the organizational agenda. It's a good idea to be aware of the type of people and events that trigger difficult behaviour patterns in you. It's also good to be aware of the shadow side of your preferred leadership roles, because that's the type of behaviour you may be prone to displaying under stress. The suggestions provided by Heifetz offer a useful reminder for leaders facing criticism, conflict, ambiguity, pressure, stress or complexity; and that's most of us!

Part 5

Resources for developing others

15

Useful exercises for groups and teams

This chapter offers ways of using the five roles to stimulate learning and discussion in traditional management development courses, experiential leadership programmes or management team workshops. The exercises below are designed to enable participants to identify which roles they need to develop, and provide opportunities for both active and reflective learning.

In a traditional management development course, the five-roles model can provide a good basis for participants to examine, practise and develop the ways in which they show up as leaders. If the participants are currently in leadership positions, they can explore the type of leadership that's needed in the current context versus the type of leadership they are providing. It's useful also to imagine possible future scenarios and encourage leaders to experiment with new ways of approaching tricky situations.

In an experiential leadership programme, which typically involves a mixture of assignments, exercises and secondments, the five roles can provide a way for the participant to reflect on his or her development as the programme progresses. This can be done by exploring the natural leadership roles each participant takes and the leadership roles that he or she needs to understand better and try out more often.

In a management team workshop, it's possible to go even further than this; the team can explore how and in what proportions leadership is taken by the various players round the table, what the organization currently needs from them as a team and what roles they need to develop collectively and individually.

Session 1: Part of traditional management development course (two hours)

- Ask everyone to complete the self-assessment questionnaire in Chapter 12. (10 mins)
- Tell people to put away the questionnaire and listen. Go through the five-roles model using flipcharts or slides. Use the material in Chapter 3, and include some of your own examples, preferably using some culturally familiar leaders to provide colour and interest. You might also use one or two film clips (eg *Henry V* for the Visionary Motivator, *Twelve Angry Men* for the Edgy Catalyst). (20–30 mins)
- Get people to guess themselves, and produce a pie chart that represents how frequently they have used each of the five roles over the past year. See Figure 15.1 for an example of this. (10 mins)

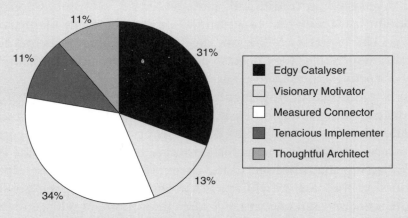

Figure 15.1 Leader's frequency pie chart for use of five leadership roles

- Invite participants to compare their self-assessment questionnaire results with their own 'guess' for themselves. Ask participants to discuss in threes a) how all this information is landing with them (excited, disappointed, disinterested), b) which leadership roles their current situation needs from them, c) next steps for them (eg inquiry, practice, develop, obtain feedback etc). (20 mins)
- Set up a role practice exercise: Put five different-coloured A4 sheets out on the floor, each with the name of one of the five roles on it. Each sheet should be placed at one of the five apexes of a very large imaginary pentagon. Ask all participants to gather at the centre. Ask each participant to name one role that they would like to experiment with (this reflection is for their own benefit!). Take each of the following situations in turn.
  - You would like you and your partner to emigrate to the other side of the world together.
  - You want to encourage your boss to invest in a new scheme for the department.
  - You think the team need to learn French to deal with a new client team.
  - You wish to inspire this team of volunteer town-centre environmentalists.
  - Get people engaged in your latest pet project.
  - Get the team together to clean up the office this weekend.

  For each one, describe the situation, and ask the participants to move quickly to the place that represents the leadership stance they want to take in this situation (it doesn't have to be the 'right' answer). Invite a few people to play an exaggerated version of the role they chose, in the situation described (remind people that the body learns through exaggeration). Get reactions from others in the group, especially regarding the effects felt by potential followers in response to leadership stances. (40 mins)

Session 2: Part of experiential leadership programme (two hours)

- Send participants a copy of this book to read. Ask them to read the five role chapters before they come to the next session, trying to place themselves in relation to all five roles (Part 2).

- In the session, ask participants to draw out three leadership role pie charts. The first pie chart should represent the proportions in which they used each of the five roles in their previous leadership role. The second chart should represent the proportions for their current leadership role, and the third chart should represent how they would like to approach their next leadership role (maybe a promotion, or a different area). Ask them to compare their own charts with someone else whom they perceive to have a different style from them and notice the similarities and differences. Are the differences and similarities to do with background, personality or context? (20 mins)

- Invite participants to examine Figure 11.1, which illustrates which roles are likely to be most successful for which organizational change contexts. Put participants in twos to discuss how well they have matched role to context as a leader over the past few years, and to draw three conclusions about their own use of the five roles (one past-focused, one present-focused and one future-focused conclusion). (20 mins)

- Hold a plenary discussion to draw out the conclusions. (10 mins)

- Ask participants to work in threes to generate and act out three pairs of sketches. Each pair of sketches allows one of the participants to demonstrate the type of leadership he or she would like to role-model, firstly in an ideally matched situation (eg a Visionary Motivator with an eager crowd), and then in a situation which is quite difficult to deal with (eg an Edgy Catalyser with a room of people who are half-asleep). These can be quite comical and wild if you like. (30 mins)

- Invite each group of three to 'perform' their two best sketches to the rest of the group. Don't discuss these – just watch. Encourage applause! (15 mins)

- After all the sketches are done, sit in a circle and give everyone the time and space to share comments about what that exercise triggered in them, and what this experience means for them and their own quest to be a more effective leader. (25 mins)

Session 3: Part of management team workshop (two hours)

- Create five colourful flipcharts, each of which summarizes one of the five leadership roles. Include some elements of the shadow side, and one or two pointers from the research. Place these flipcharts on stands around the room.

- Talk through the five leadership roles, explaining how they were derived, and pointing out that effective leadership involves using all five roles in various strengths. Include your own examples of the roles and invite them to think of local examples of each role. (15 mins)

- Get each management team member to produce a pie chart that represents how frequently they have used each of the five roles over the past year. See Figure 15.1 for an example of this. If participants know each other well enough, ask them to guess each other's role profiles, naming the two roles they think are used most frequently by each team member. Ask team members to create two Post-It notes for each team member, writing the leadership role and the person's name on each sticker, and invite everyone to stick these Post-It notes on the relevant flipcharts. (20 mins)

- Facilitate a discussion that allows each leader in the group to hear how others see his/her leadership and openly compare this with his/her perception of self. Note that in management teams there may be a difference between how an individual is experienced at management team meetings versus how they are seen to lead their own teams. (30 mins)

- Move from examining individual styles to exploring the collective approach used by the team. Ask each team member to draw a role profile for the team, using the same pie-chart approach. (5 mins)

- Then ask one member of the team (not the traditional leader) to facilitate a discussion in which they agree on a pie chart that represents how their leadership approach has been as a management team over the past 1–2 years. (20 mins)

- Using Figure 11.1 as a prompt, facilitate a discussion in which the team define the current organizational context (key shifts required in the organization, important deliverables, etc) and draw a pie chart of the leadership profile required by the organizational context. Then discuss the match between the profile of the team and the profile that's needed. Agree three actions to improve the quality of this match. (30 mins)

MORE SHORT EXERCISES TO EXPLORE THE FIVE ROLES

1. Ask participants to think about:
    - their last important meeting;
    - their last family/group holiday;
    - their last work crisis;
    - their last party/celebration.

    Questions to consider:
    - How would someone using the Edgy Catalyser, Visionary Motivator, Measured Connector, Tenacious Implementer, Thoughtful Architect roles approach this situation? Tackle each situation, looking at one role at a time.
    - How did you approach the situation?
    - Do you notice any patterns? If so, what are your conclusions?

2. Invite participants to think about each of the following people in their lives and rate the ability of these people to use each of the five leadership roles from 0 to 5:
    - current boss;
    - deputy (or similar);
    - previous boss;
    - partner/best mate;
    - CEO;
    - main rival in work or life;
    - self.

3. Encourage participants to ask their coach/mentor/boss/critical friend to list the participant's three strengths and three weaknesses for each of the five roles. Invite the participant to choose two strengths to focus on and two weaknesses to work on.

4. Ask participants to name their three favourite superheroes (eg Spiderman, Batgirl, the fairy godmother). Then ask: 'If you were each one, which leadership role would you use the most?'

    This exercise should tell participants something about their leadership aspirations.

5. Ask participants to name their three least favourite 'popular leaders' (eg Richard Branson, Alan Sugar, Donald Trump). Which of the five leadership roles do they use the most?

This exercise should tell participants something about their shadow side as a leader.

6. Ask each participant to review the last team meeting he or she ran and consider which roles other team members played. Participants need to use their own words for these: one adjective and one noun, eg grumpy child, reticent professor, forthright fact-gatherer, repetitive salesman, calm healer. Ask the participant to reflect on how he/she responds to each of these roles. For example, when someone acts like a grumpy child, I tend to become a critical schoolteacher in response, whereas if someone acts like a calm healer, I become a passive learner.

    This exercise explores the idea of a 'role dance'. In a 'role dance' we respond to the roles that others take in a sometimes predictable, and often unhelpful, way.

7. Ask participants to work in small groups. Ask each participant to talk about their current leadership challenges for 10 minutes. These should be specific rather than general, eg get a project that has drifted off schedule on track, deal with poor morale in the customer care team. The other participants listen without asking questions, and then respond by telling the individual which leadership approach they think needs to be used and why.

8. Ask each participant to consider each of the five roles and think of a time they successfully stepped into that role in an organizational, family or community situation. Get them to recollect how they felt, what they saw, what they heard etc and see if they can re-create the bodily sensations of being successful in that role. Get them to 'anchor' this by associating the sensation with a word or phrase (eg 'Edgy Catalyser') or gesture.

16

The roles in action

This chapter looks at how the five leadership roles can be used from a range of positions in the organizational hierarchy. Leadership is not merely the preserve of senior management; we believe that leadership needs to be present at all levels within an organization if that organization is to be successful. So if we take the view that leadership is about 'recognizing and responding to the challenges facing us in our organizations and communities' (Pedlar *et al*, 2004), then it is possible for anyone to step into a leadership role whenever and wherever there is a need.

Here, we will look at stepping into the five roles when you are a senior manager, a middle manager or a member of staff. We will also explore the use of the five roles when you are a dedicated change manager, responsible for coordinating or directing change initiatives, or a partnership worker, building business partnerships or local community partnerships.

THE SENIOR MANAGER

Much of the literature about leadership focuses on senior management activity, and this book is no exception. However, it is important to remember the dynamics at work within organizations. The work of

Oshry (1996) is a good reminder of the propensity for senior managers to see themselves as responsible for everything, with a tendency to keep decision making and information sharing too close to the centre, thus making it difficult for others to take their share of the responsibility and relieve the burden.

Oshry highlights the need for senior people in organizations to make it possible for those who work for them to become leaders in their own right. This means rewarding, inspiring, connecting, informing and developing others. In terms of the five leadership roles, these are the types of activities required:

- Focus on problems and issues, but don't solve things for people (Edgy Catalyser).

- Inspire others to give their energies to completing the task, don't just tell them to do it (Visionary Motivator).

- Become a good sponsor, understanding a variety of agendas and enabling people to connect with each other (Measured Connector).

- Commit resources to the change; don't just ask people to squeeze things in amongst the day-job (Tenacious Implementer).

- Develop a clear design for the organization so that people can see where they fit in (Thoughtful Architect).

THE MIDDLE MANAGER

Middle managers have an increasingly difficult role within organizations. They have to deal with the tensions between the high-level strategic vision and the practical implications of this. Theorists often differentiate between what managers do and what leaders do, but in the case of middle managers, there is a need to be both leader and manager, translating the strategic into the operational and feeding ideas back up the line.

Middle managers often experience multiple demands on their time, receiving many conflicting requests from different parts of the organization, which can become quite debilitating. Caught in this maze of different agendas, they can start to be seen as indecisive and inefficient;

often referred to as the 'soggy sponge' or the 'clay layer' of the organization, perceived by senior managers as resistant to change and described as weak and ineffective. However, middle managers can really help to move the organization forward if they remember to:

- Push back to senior management on some of their more crazy ideas while spotting what's working and what's not in the operational areas (Edgy Catalyser).

- Translate the vision into inspiring language and be an enthusiastic role model for change, if you believe it (Visionary Motivator).

- Become the bridge between the overarching organizational objectives and the tangible tasks for their staff; link across the organization to create real joined-up thinking; keep close to directors and to staff (Measured Connector).

- Ensure that information is passed from operations to the centre and vice versa. Insist that planning and performance management systems work and that what gets measured gets done. Protect projects from the vagaries of senior management (Tenacious Implementer).

- Understand where the team adds value to the overall vision. Design local processes that work (Thoughtful Architect).

THE MEMBER OF STAFF

Staff can feel disregarded and ignored, especially during times of organizational change. They feel vulnerable and 'done to', and the idea of taking responsibility and showing leadership themselves becomes quite a distant concept. If you are a member of staff, it will help you to escape the uncomfortable sensation of vulnerability if you try to become someone who is responsible for your own situation, and someone who takes responsibility for moving the whole organization forward in some way.

- Ask questions about why things are done the way they are, especially when you think something is inefficient. You may have to temper your words and find skilful routes to get your message across. But you might have a good point, and at least you will make people think (Edgy Catalyser).

- If something is not right, inspire the others around you to help you to do something about it. Propose new ways of working. Take action and ask for forgiveness later. Try to align your own personal goals with the organizational goals. If you can do this, you will not only enjoy your time at work better, you'll inspire people around you (Visionary Motivator).

- Find out who's who and what everyone's agenda is; include your internal customers, bosses, internal suppliers and key stakeholders. This will be useful both to you and to your colleagues in the long run (Measured Connector).

- Ensure that the job you are doing is really adding value to the organization and that you are doing it as efficiently and effectively as possible (Tenacious Implementer).

- Study the core processes involved in your work, collect important data, and encourage others to work with you to understand who does what and how things work – this can result in breakthrough thinking as regards improved ways of working (Thoughtful Architect).

THE CHANGE MANAGER

The change manager has a difficult job on his or her hands, involving many different facets of leadership. Typically, a change manager is responsible for the delivery of a number of connected projects, or for the progression of a more complex organizational shift such as a culture change or a merger. This role generally features a tricky mix of high levels of accountability and visibility without very much authority.

In any change initiative it's important that the leaders involved are able to juggle various different organizational areas of focus. In Chapter 4 we referred to these areas of focus as:

- Discomfort – what's not working at the moment and who knows about this? Where is this organization hurting?

- Buy-in – how is it possible to harness the human resources and talent around the organization, and inspire, motivate and engage people?

- Connectivity – how do we ensure that the organization knows enough about itself and its purpose and competencies and is well connected enough to be able to self-organize and change in a healthy responsive way when it needs to?

- Projects – what needs to be done to manage key projects and ensure all the necessary resources are acquired, the projects are delivered on time, to budget and to the right quality?

- Design – what are the structural and process designs for the future?

The change manager is often given the role of ensuring that change happens, therefore he or she needs to be able to influence the right people, in the right way, at the right time. These five areas of organizational focus are an important guide for the change manager to direct his or her energies.

So change managers need to:

- Ensure that all those who need to put effort into making the change happen understand why it's important, and where the organizational pain is now (Edgy Catalyser).

- Envisage the future state of the organization, and be able to 'sell' this to the various stakeholders, especially those who haven't been involved from the beginning of the initiative (Visionary Motivator).

- Remind the change team of the organization's purpose – especially if this has changed – and enable the right people to get together to sort out the complex or intractable issues (Measured Connector).

- Plan the various change activities, get the right resources in place and ensure that the plan is implemented; include other, less obvious areas of the organization in the planning process, such as business management, communications, office management, training, HR etc (Tenacious Implementer).

- Think through the more complex aspects of the change process, eg provide an operating model for the new way of working or define the culture change required (Thoughtful Architect).

PARTNERSHIP WORKER

With the breaking down of organizational barriers through outsourcing, 'district-ization' or de-centralization, partnership working and stakeholder involvement, a new form of leadership is being called for. Often no single person has the authority to command and control what others decide and do. New ways of working are emerging, which span organizations and reach out to suppliers, customers, partners and the community at large.

Stepping into a leadership role in these circumstances can be very different. The 'push' style of influencing which is most directive – telling people what to do – works best with power, and needs some kind of enforcement. It can be high risk and usually gets low commitment. Often perceived as a win/lose strategy, it is typically used in more hierarchical organizations. It does have its uses of course – in crises for example, though usually effective only in the short term.

The 'pull' style is probably more useful in true partnership working as it tends to be successful even without power. Instead it requires engaging and involving people and creating an invitation for collaboration. As such it tends to be low risk and gets high commitment. It's based on the principle of win/win and is most effective over the long term.

- Although there's always a place for the Edgy Catalyser in getting people to be aware of where the issues are, the role needs to be handled carefully when you have no control over the person. The Edgy Catalyser role will be useful for gently raising fundamental problems.

- In contrast, the Visionary Motivator role is one which can really cross organizational boundaries, inspiring people, and building energized cross-functional teams. But partnership workers need to remember that the ultimate vision has to be shared and commonly understood.

- The Measured Connector is perhaps a natural role for cross-boundary working. This task is difficult if there are rigid organizational boundaries between key partners that have been in existence for years. Nonetheless, the Measured Connector is good at spotting the people that matter in the context of the whole system, and bringing them together in meaningful ways.

- The Tenacious Implementer can sometimes have a hard job when the people in the team have dual accountabilities and split loyalties. It's difficult enough in a matrix organization for a Tenacious Implementer to feel the satisfaction of making something actually happen. Working with a myriad of stakeholders can be like trying to knit jelly. It's very frustrating, and it often seems impossible to progress any decision or activity when faced with people from different organizations, different cultures, uncertain resources and conflicting accounting periods. The Tenacious Implementer is a very important role in this context, because it's very easy for people to meet and talk and get lost in the complexity of it all, without anything ever being achieved or agreed.

- The Thoughtful Architect will have their work cut out to forge a conceptual map which encompasses the different wants and needs of all partner organizations. However, developing a common model is critical, and understanding how multiple objectives can be linked and locked is an extremely sophisticated task, most effectively achieved by the Thoughtful Architect.

Epilogue

In writing this book, we have tried to create a practical manual for managers (and people in other walks of life), which will enable them to more easily step into the different roles they choose or life throws at them. We wanted to create a book which saw leadership from a slightly different perspective from previous research, and even more importantly, we wanted to highlight the fact that taking up a role doesn't have to be the most difficult thing in the world.

Clearly, because of your own unique mix of personality, background, education and training, and organizational situation, you probably fit more or less easily into some of the leadership roles than others. That's ok. The aspiration is to have ways of stepping into those roles if you need to and ensuring that others around you can do so too, if you, for whatever reason, can't. The point is not to get too hung up about the roles you *should* be playing but to play around a little with the roles you *could* step into or perhaps the roles you *choose* to step into.

The underlying philosophy of this book is not that each and every one of us can be all things to all people. We do not subscribe to the view that you only need to be positive, think positive and act positive to be the person you aspire to. Our philosophy is that deep within ourselves we have untapped possibilities and talents and that by stepping into roles – not necessarily having to be different – we can expand our repertoire of behaviour, actions and results. We do not have to limit ourselves by either self-perception or self-conception, or by what others might care to think of us.

I don't know whether you have had the experience of finding it easy to change the way you are when you enter different circumstances – for example, being able to give up smoking when you start in a new job because no one has labelled you as a 'smoker'. Likewise you may be more able to step into a team leader role on a Monday when you aren't managing people with whom you went out socializing the Friday night before. So by practising the roles through trying the exercises in this book, you should be able to free both body and mind a little more easily.

Life's journey constantly gives you the opportunity to step into new roles without prior training. Team leaders tend to get promoted because of their ability to do the job directly below; becoming a parent for the first time doesn't come with a manual of everything to do in every eventuality. You often have to make it up as you go along. It's called life, and that's the challenge.

We can all prepare ourselves for these challenges; we have our experiences of being managed, or of being parented. But often these are quite limited. There are many ways of being managed, and an infinite number of ways of being parented. Trying things on for size, based on your experience, the experiences of others, what the research says and with a little feedback from friends, colleagues and a coach or mentor, is perhaps as good a way as any of stepping into these roles.

We hope that we've struck the right balance between offering some academic rigour and a practical and pragmatic approach to what leaders actually do in the field. Having reviewed the literature and reflected upon our many years of practice in the field of change consultancy and leadership development, we spoke to scores of people before developing the five leadership roles. We then tested these roles out with a further 80 managers to see if the roles passed the 'practitioner test'. They did.

Yes, leadership is about personality; it is about characteristics and traits; it is about management and leadership competencies. It is about having a style of leadership for a given set of circumstances. Leadership impacts and is impacted by other people – their motivation and their competence. Leadership is about operating in a specific culture, within a specific organization; and it is about responding to different organizational change situations. But it is also very much about identifying what role the leader needs to play given the change challenge. Our research clearly show that different roles are more useful in certain situations, and a combination of roles for specific change situations is seen to be more effective in leading change.

Some years ago I was working with a client, setting up one of the UK's first 24-hour contact centres. I was amazed by, and somewhat in awe of, the level of boundless energy, drive and visionary zeal that the operations manager had. He excelled at the Visionary Motivator role. I was intrigued that someone could have so much energy, so clear a vision, and to do this so naturally. And strangely, some of the seeds for this book were sown when I discovered, over many a long discussion with him, the lengths he needed to go to in order to keep his passion and energy going. It was a part of him; he was being authentic and genuine, but he needed to prepare himself every day to step seamlessly into that role. The organization's vision and values helped; his own boss helped; the people he recruited to work with all helped. His personality helped (ENTP if you are a Myers Briggs person!). But each morning he consciously had to step into that role. Likewise in the long and detailed negotiations with the software supplier he had to step into the role of Tenacious Implementer. He had others for support, but the need for persistence, perseverance and quite specific objectives left him no option but to play the role for all that he was worth.

When Disney staff step into the park they step into their role; the role of entertainer. When employees from a mobile-phone business step out of the stock room into the shop, they are stepping into their role – professional, courteous, considerate. When you take on the role of leadership you are stepping into that role as well. The ethos of this book is that you need to consciously choose the nature of the role you play.

We have drawn upon various frameworks and techniques to identify the steps that you need to take in order to play these roles to the best of your ability. The roles need flexing. Your personality, your skill set, your level of confidence will all play a part in the ease with which you may step into these roles. We urge you to take these first steps and also to let us know how you get on. We'd appreciate hearing about your experiences of the five roles – observed in others and performed by yourselves. We're keen to strike up a dialogue to discover what works and what can be enhanced. Please do contact us on the e-mail addresses below.

In the meantime, best wishes for your leadership practice!

Esther Cameron   Mike Green
www.cameronchange.co.uk   www.transitionalspace.co.uk
esther@cameronchange.co.uk   mike@transitionalspace.co.uk

Please keep a look out on both our websites for slide packs, trainer guides and workshop paraphernalia, which are all currently under development.

References

PART 1: INTRODUCTION

Adair, J (2004) *The John Adair Handbook of Management and Leadership*, Thorogood, London

Bass, B M and Avolio, B J (1990) Developing transformational leadership, *Journal of European Industrial Training*, **14** (5), pp 21–27

Belbin, M (1981) *Teams: Why they succeed or fail*, Butterworth-Heinemann, London

Bennis, W G (1994) *On Becoming a Leader*, Addison-Wesley, Reading, MA

Bennis, W G (1996) The leader as storyteller, *Harvard Business Review*, **74** (1), pp 154–61

Bennis, W G and Nanus, B (1985) *Leadership: Strategies for taking charge*, Harper & Row, New York

Binney, G and Williams, L (1995) *Leaning into the Future*, Nicholas Brealey, London

Blake, R R and Mouton, J S (1985) *The Managerial Grid: The key to leadership excellence*, Gulf Publishing Co, Houston, TX

Cameron, E and Green, M (2004) *Making Sense of Change Management*, Kogan Page, London

Covey, S (1989) *The Seven Habits of Highly Effective People*, Simon & Schuster, London

Covey, S (1992) *Principle-Centered Leadership*, Simon & Schuster, London

Farkas, C M and Wetlaufer, S (1996) The ways chief executive officers lead, *Harvard Business Review*, **74** (3), pp 110–22

Goleman, D (2000) Leadership that gets results, *Harvard Business Review*, **78** (2), 78–91

George, B (2004) *Authentic Leadership*, Jossey Bass, San Francisco

Heifetz, R (1994) *Leadership Without Easy Answers*, Harvard University Press, Boston, MA

Hersey, P and Blanchard, K (1988) *Management of Organizational Behaviour*, Prentice-Hall, Englewood Cliffs, NJ

Hind, P (1999) Leader abilities, directions, *The Ashridge Journal*, April, Ashridge Business School

Kanter, R (1999) The enduring skills of change leaders, *Leader to Leader*, Issue 13

Kotter, J P (1990) What leaders really do, *Harvard Business Review*, **68** (3), pp 103–12

Kotter, J P (1996) *Leading Change*, Harvard Business School Press, Boston, MA

Lipman-Blumen, J (2002) The age of connective leadership, in *On Leading Change*, ed F Hesselbein and R Johnston, pp 89–102, Jossey-Bass, New York

Northouse, P (2004) *Leadership Theory and Practice*, 3rd edn, Sage, Thousand Oaks, CA

Sadler, P (2003) *Leadership*, Kogan Page, London

Senge, P (1993) *The Fifth Discipline*, Nicolas Brealey, London

Senge, P *et al* (1999) *The Dance of Change*, Nicolas Brealey, London

Stogdill, R M (1974) *Handbook of Leadership*, The Free Press, New York

Syrett, M and Hogg, C (1993) *Frontiers of Leadership*, Blackwell, Oxford

Tannenbaum, R and Schmidt, W H (1973), How to choose a leadership pattern, *Harvard Business Review*, **51** (3), pp 162–80

Tichy, N M and Devanna, M A (1986) *The Transformational Leaders*, Wiley, New York

Wheatley, M (1993) *Leadership and the New Science*, Berrett-Koehler, San Francisco

PART 2: UNDERSTANDING THE FIVE ROLES

Birkinshaw, J and Crainer, S (2002) *Leadership the Sven-Goran Eriksson Way*, Capstone, Oxford

Campbell, A (2007) *The Blair Years*, Hutchinson, London

Gladwell, M (2002) *The Tipping Point: How little things can make a big difference*, Back Bay Books, Boston, MA

Goleman, D (1998) *Working with Emotional Intelligence*, Bloomsbury, London

Goth, B (2007) In on a stallion, out with tail between legs, *Washington Post*, 16 May, available at: http://hanua.blogspot.com/2007_05_13_ archive.html

Schultz, H (1997) *Pour Your Heart Into It*, Hyperion, New York

Scott, S (2002) *Fierce Conversations*, Piatkus, London

Senge, P *et al* (2004) *Presence*, Cambridge University Press, New York

Smit, T (2002) *Eden*, Corgi Books, London

Soros, G (1987) *The Alchemy of Finance*, John Wiley & Sons, New York

Troy, G (2005) *Morning in America: How Ronald Reagan invented the 1980s*, Politics and Society in Twentieth-Century America Series, Princeton University Press, Princeton, NJ

PART 3: THE RESEARCH

Aiello, R J and Watkins, M D (2000) The fine art of friendly acquisition, *Harvard Business Review*, **78** (6), pp 101–07

Cameron, E (2007) What a song and dance, *The Guardian*, Wednesday 18 April

Cohen, J (1988) *Statistical Power Analysis for the Behavioral Sciences*, Erlbaum, Hillsdale, NJ

Handy, C (1989) *The Age of Unreason*, Business Books, London

Kotter, J (1995) Leading change: why transformation efforts fail, *Harvard Business Review*, **73** (2), pp 59–67

PART 4: EXPANDING YOUR REPERTOIRE

Cameron, E and Green, M (2004) *Making Sense of Change Management*, Kogan Page, London

de Bono, E (1985) *Six Thinking Hats*, Little, Brown, Boston, MA

Egan (1994) *Working the Shadow Side*, Jossey-Bass, San Francisco

Hagen, U (1973) *Respect for Acting*, Macmillan, New York

Heifetz, R (1994) *Leadership Without Easy Answers*, Harvard University Press, Boston, MA

Rasiel, E M and Friga, P N (2001) *The McKinsey Mind*, McGraw-Hill Professional, Maidenhead

Vygotsky, L S (1978) *Mind in Society*, Harvard University Press, Cambridge, MA

Zweig, C and Abrams, J (1990) *Meeting the Shadow: Hidden power of the dark side of human nature*, Tarcher/Putnam, New York

PART 5: RESOURCES FOR DEVELOPING OTHERS

Oshry, B (1996) *Seeing Systems*, Berrett-Koehler, San Francisco

Pedlar, M *et al* (2004) *A Manager's Guide to Leadership*, McGraw-Hill UK, Maidenhead

Index

NB: page numbers in *italic* indicate drawings, figures and tables